vintage fabric style

vintage fabric style

stylish ideas and projects using quilts
and flea-market finds in your home

LUCINDA GANDERTON

ROSE HAMMICK

WITH PHOTOGRAPHY BY **CATHERINE GRATWICKE**

RYLAND
PETERS
& SMALL

LONDON NEW YORK

Senior designer **Sally Powell**

Senior editors **Sophie Bevan**, **Henrietta Heald**

Location and picture researcher **Emily Westlake**

Production director **Meryl Silbert**

Art director **Gabriella Le Grazie**

Publishing director **Alison Starling**

Text and projects **Lucinda Ganderton**

Styling **Rose Hammick**

Illustrations **Lizzie Sanders**

Proofreader and indexer **Alison Bravington**

First published in the USA in 2003
by Ryland Peters & Small, Inc.
519 Broadway
5th Floor
New York, NY 10012
www.rylandpeters.com

Library of Congress Cataloging-in-Publication Data

Ganderton, Lucinda.
  Vintage fabric style : inspirational ideas for using antique and retro
fabrics in your home / by Lucinda Ganderton and Rose Hammick.
      p. cm.
Includes index.
  ISBN 1-84172-416-5
  1. Household linens. 2. Textile fabrics in interior decoration. 3. Textile fabrics--
Conservation and restoration. 4. Vintage clothing. I. Hammick, Rose. II. Title.
  TT387 .G35 2003
  746.9--dc21
                                                          2002015785

contents

introduction

Vintage fabric style is an essentially eclectic approach to living. It can be quirky, classic, opulent, minimalist, or chic, but it is always individual, and no two people will interpret it in the same way. By taking the best of the past and mixing it with the new, you can create a modern style that transcends fashion and the quick makeover—and which is equally at home in a rural cabin, a city brownstone, or an industrial loft space.

In the same way that architects and designers incorporate the rich pickings of the salvage yard into new homes, you can reclaim antique textiles and give them a new life in new settings. There is an intriguing domestic heritage of clothing, lace, curtains, quilts, and cushions just waiting to be discovered and re-used—a legacy of several generations of women who had the time and skill to seek out and make decorative items for their own households.

Developments in the way we decorate our homes reflect the way we live just as much as changes in the clothes we wear. Vintage furnishings, linens, and needlework vary tremendously

in style and scale, and you are bound to find an historical look that appeals to you. Whether you prefer Victorian floral chintzes, embroidered bags and beaded pincushions, handwoven cotton sheets, or the bold geometrics of the 1950s and 1960s, there is something uniquely satisfying about living with one-off pieces that have survived the years.

Running through the decades is the theme of sewing as a craft of economic necessity, which flourished particularly at times when new materials were expensive or unobtainable. In a spirit of "make do and mend," curtains have always been lengthened or shortened to fit new windows, worn tablecloths turned into napkins, and adult clothing cut down and made into children's wear—and it is this kind of innovative adaptation that lies at the heart of many of the interiors featured in the following chapters.

This book aims to introduce you to a new way of looking at old textiles—by putting them into your own setting, altering and changing them as necessary, you can create a personal style that has a timeless quality. As the character of the new century becomes established, vintage has never been so contemporary.

LUCINDA GANDERTON

hunting &
gathering

Building up a collection of fabrics and antique accessories is great fun—and the hunt for that elusive but essential one-off item will probably give you as much pleasure as actually using it or transforming it into something new. There is no need to take the process too seriously. You are not aiming to recreate an historic period or a small-scale version of a country house—the look isn't coordinated and tailored, so follow your instincts, have confidence in your own style, and buy pieces that you like and will enjoy living with.

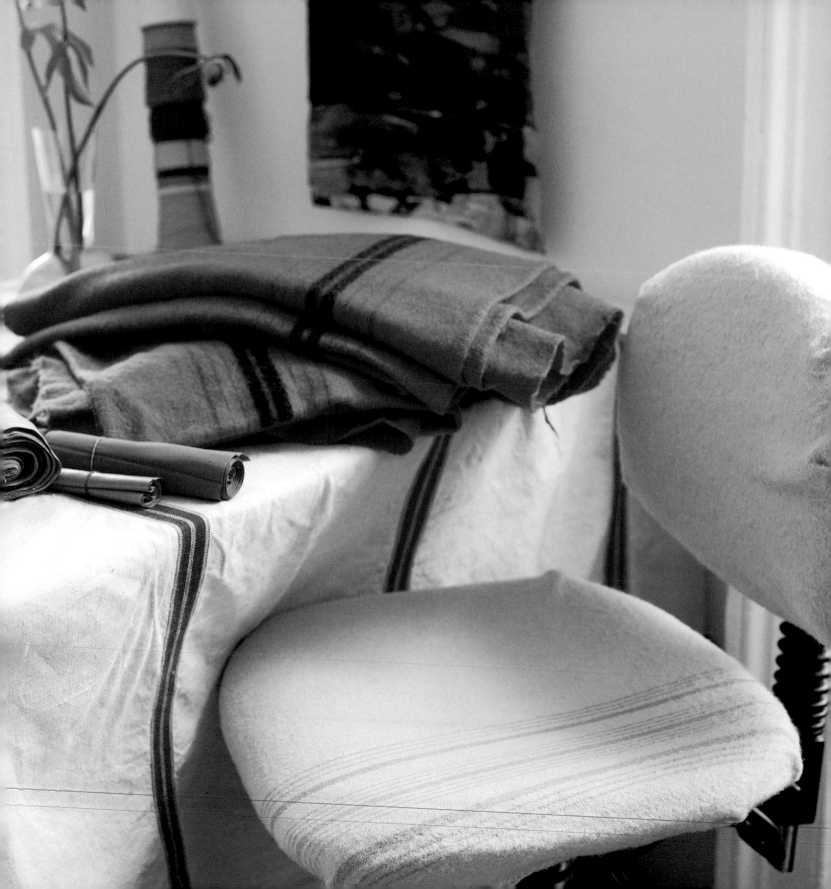

When you begin your quest for vintage fabrics, you'll find a wealth of sources waiting to be investigated. At the top end of the market, leading auction houses hold regular sales of historic textiles including fans, quilts, costumes, and lace, many of museum quality. But, with a bit of determination, you can unearth everyday treasures in thrift shops, flea markets, and yard sales.

OPPOSITE This sturdy cabinet offers ideal storage: the glass-paneled doors allow folded stacks of interesting linens to be kept on view, but protected from dust, while the drawers and cupboards below provide ample space for other items.

LEFT If you mimic Victorian schoolchildren by using slate and a piece of chalk to label open wicker baskets, you can check the contents at a glance.

RIGHT Most of your collection can be kept on shelves and in closets, but some things, such as this floaty lawn dress, are just too pretty to hide away.

Apart from general antique shops, which often have a few bits and pieces, there are many specialized dealers in vintage clothing, textiles and accessories who carry wide-ranging stock. Look for Venetian beads, crocheted doilies, spools of silk ribbon, old shoe laces, buttons on their original cards, lace edged handkerchiefs, silk flowers, christening gowns, and cards of rick-rack braid. Some dealers have their own shops (listed in local trade directories); others deal from stands in arcades or flea markets. Many also exhibit at the major fairs around the country, which are advertised in listings and collectors' magazines.

Local auctions or dealers whose main business is house clearance often have job lots of linen and curtains, which can be bought at knockdown prices. Search through these at the open viewing with a keen eye for any overlooked treasure.

BELOW An assortment of antique steel scissors and an old tape measure make an unusual display that can also be put to practical use when you are stitching.

RIGHT A dress form or a dressmaker's dummy is a companionable presence in the sewing room. This model is adjustable to suit different figures—or to accommodate an expanding waistline!

LEFT When you get your haul back home, wash and press the fabrics, then put them into piles of similar colors and patterns, ready to be used or simply to be looked at and enjoyed.

FAR LEFT A set of small drawers or an apothecary chest is a useful piece of furniture that gives you lots of room for storing little items in an orderly way. Old and new cottons in vibrant primary shades are kept together here for easy access.

You may be lucky enough to have a grandmother or greataunt who is not only a talented needlewoman, but also an inveterate hoarder. You might just find an understairs cupboard or attic filled with a lifetime's stockpile of notions, and a library of needlework encyclopedias, knitting books, and old magazines, complete with giveaway iron-on transfer patterns.

Most households have at least a battered tin of buttons, beads, zippers, and forgotten broken necklaces. Even the most unpromising boxes of old bricabrac can yield unused remnants of 1950s dressmaking prints, once-treasured satin wedding shoes, linen towels, or embroidered traycloths.

Wash and iron everything as soon as you can, to get rid of any musty aroma. If you have a magpie's instincts, you won't need to be told to salvage the best bits—buttons, buckles, braid, lace, and beading, or woven labels, monograms, and embroidery—from pieces that are worn or damaged beyond repair. The true collector loves to be surrounded by beautiful objects—so, once you have accumulated your hoard, keep the best pieces on display and enjoy their various textures, colors, and patterns.

You can continue the hunt when traveling, either at home or abroad. A *murché aux puces* (flea market) or provincial *brocante* fair may yield offbeat souvenirs. To be truly international without even leaving home, try the internet. There are many websites run by antique dealers, and using the internet may be the quickest way to track down a 1930s feedsack or an original pioneer quilt, for example.

OPPOSITE, ABOVE LEFT These industrial cones of jute and linen on their original cardboard spools may have been used for weaving, while the round balls are of lustrous crochet thread.

OPPOSITE, BELOW LEFT Print chests, once used to store metal type, have tiers of drawers divided into many small compartments, making them ideal for storing fabric samples and scraps.

OPPOSITE, RIGHT Tucked into the eaves, this sunny sewing room has an intimate feel, conducive to creativity. Boxes and baskets are hidden away below the work surface behind the striped curtain, while smaller items are kept in the wooden and plastic drawers.

ABOVE Keep your spools of thread and needlework tools at hand in open baskets and shallow work boxes. The colors of old sewing threads are muted and softer than many of those produced today.

ABOVE RIGHT The geometric pattern of the glass dish complements the iridescent texture of these mother-of-pearl buttons and the design on the cream Art Deco-style buttons.

A needle and thread is all you need for most basic sewing, but a well-stocked workbasket will provide the equipment needed for embroidering, patching, darning, and creating new items from your antique fabrics. If you are starting from scratch, invest in the best kit to help you to achieve lasting and professional results. Look out, too, for old needlework tools—thimbles, pincushions, needlecases, or spool holders, which are enjoyable to work with and to collect.

It is useful to have several pairs of scissors, each kept for its own purpose. Dressmaking shears with long blades and angled handles are for cutting out and should be kept sharp. Pinking shears give a nonfray zigzag edge. Sewing scissors are smaller and have straight handles. Use these for notching seam allowances and clipping

corners but never for paper, which will blunt them. You may come across old steel embroidery scissors, still ideal for trimming and unpicking.

Hand-sewing needles come in different sizes for various tasks. Medium-length "sharps" are for general sewing and basting, and shorter "betweens" can be used for slip stitch and quilting. Crewel needles have an extra-long eye designed for embroidery threads, while tapestry needles are blunt with a wide eye for wool yarns. The best way to store needles is in a

needlebook, with a felt page for each type. There's even a choice of pins: stainless steel dressmaker's pins can be used for most fabrics and brass lace-making pins for finer cloth, while glass-headed pins are best for wool and other thick material.

A thimble will protect your finger when basting long seams, quilting, or handstitching patchwork pieces; if you haven't used one before, it may take a while to get used to. They come in different sizes, so find one that fits snugly on your middle finger.

When buying sewing thread, select one made from the same weight and fiber as the fabric to be stitched. Mercerized cotton has a smooth surface and should be used for cotton and linens. Polyester is finer and can be used for mixed fabrics. Match the color as closely as possible, and choose a darker shade if an exact match is not possible.

Old wooden spools of thread with antique labels are often more subtle than new ones, but check the strength before actually sewing with them because they may have become brittle over the years. You may discover antique embroidery threads, soft floss, or spools of silk in the most exquisite and irreplaceable shades, and it is difficult to resist using them. Look

FAR LEFT Skeins of embroidery floss can be taken off their paper loops and wound onto cardboard spools for ease of use.

MAIN PICTURE Pillows made from skillfully chosen combinations of old fabrics in contrasting textures wait to be dispatched to customers.

INSET A good pair of cutting-out shears with heavy steel blades is a necessary tool for everyone who stitches. You may find that they lose their sharpness if you work with a lot of pure silk, but try to use them on fabric only. If you use them to cut paper or cardboard, they will become blunt even more quickly.

out also for trimmings and keep a ragbag for scraps of lace, sequin braiding, satin cord, and fringing, along with odd buttons and beads—all of which can be incorporated into new textile pieces.

Other helpful notions are dressmaker's carbon paper or iron-on transfer paper for drawing outlines for embroidery onto fabric, interfacing to back and strengthen fine or worn fabrics, and fusible bonding web for joining fabrics and appliqué. Finally, a triangle of tailor's chalk or a dressmaker's pen is useful for marking measurements and outlines—and no sewing kit is complete without a tape measure. If you make any of the projects in the following

pages, use either standard or metric measurements— as in a recipe, the conversions are not precise.

A sewing machine is necessary if you plan to do a lot of stitching, and although the choice can be bewildering, you don't have to spend a lot of money. The latest computerized models have many advanced features, but all you really need is a basic straight stitch and maybe a zigzag for finishing seams if you are serious about fabric furnishings. Make sure the needle is sharp, and match its thickness to the weight of the fabric: the finest needles have the lowest numbers, so use size 8 for fine lawn, 12 for most cottons and linens, and size 16 for heavy canvas.

ABOVE Get comfortable for sewing—an office chair will provide good back support, and can be dressed up with a new cover for a more domestic look.

ABOVE CENTER It is satisfying to create something new from old fabrics that may not have been used for many years.

ABOVE LEFT Even a utilitarian pincushion can be a desirable object. These soft fruits, filled with cotton batt, are made from scraps of velvet in gentle, faded colors.

OPPOSITE Heaped up in baskets and hung from the studio wall, a selection of materials in all the colors of the rainbow provides inspiration for a textile artist.

living with vintage fabric

Whether you long for pared-down minimalism or prefer to surround yourself with flowered chintz, living with antique textiles is easy. Much of the pleasure that comes from decorating with old fabrics lies in the knowledge that the look you are creating will be totally unique, whatever your style. Whether you are sleeping, cooking, bathing, or sitting in the backyard, you will find there is room for a vintage influence everywhere in your home.

living rooms

In most houses and apartments, the living room is the focus of daily life. As the place where we spend most of our time—watching television, listening to music, reading, playing, eating, drinking, or relaxing with family and friends—the room is usually designed with the emphasis on comfort and enjoyment.

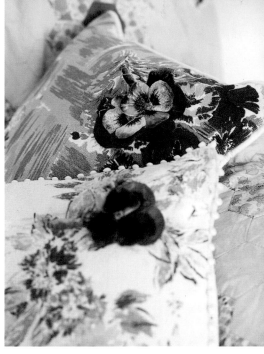

Today's comfortable living spaces and family rooms are far removed from the smart formal drawing rooms that affluent Georgians and Victorians kept for entertaining their guests.

Considered the public face of a private home, the drawing room was designed to impress with a display of fine taste in furnishings and *objets d'art*, and was used only on special occasions. In humbler dwellings, the parlor served the same purpose in more recent years.

By putting traditional elements into a new environment and placing a few vintage pieces against a contemporary backdrop, you can introduce a classic mood into your own living room. Vintage does not have to mean pastiche, and you are not seeking to recreate a period interior. The overall feel should be cool and sophisticated rather than country-cottage rustic or mock Art Deco.

Keep an open mind when looking at old fabric furnishings, and try to imagine how they could be adapted to suit a modern setting and new

ABOVE Lush velvet pansies and carefully chosen trimmings help to transform remnants of old upholstery fabrics into appealing vintage cushions.

ABOVE LEFT This traditional Grandmother's Flower Garden quilt, hand-stitched from hexagons, disguises an old armchair. On the table behind is a framed piece of lace propped informally against the wall.

LEFT A bag of material, an old sewing machine, and a stack of hatboxes make a feature of a fireplace alcove. The largest box is covered with fabric.

OPPOSITE A Trip Around the World quilt made from square patches, a wholecloth quilt, and some squashy pillows make this sofa look comfortable and inviting.

furniture. A patchwork quilt always looks right in the bedroom, but in a living room it could be dramatic draped over a sofa as a large throw, mounted on a pole as a wall hanging, or even hung at the window as a makeshift curtain. Old curtains can be tucked over armchairs as a quick alternative to slipcovers, tablecloths can be used to conceal ordinary storage boxes, and almost any piece of fabric will make a cushion or bolster cover.

You may prefer to keep color to a minimum—an abundance can make a room appear busy and too full. For a harmonious feel, and to avoid a cluttered Victorian look or a clashing 1970s pattern overload, only mix prints and designs that fall within a similar color range—and keep the background neutral where possible.

ABOVE Patterned and colored pillows in contrasting textures can be artfully used to soften the starkness of a white or pale-colored armchair.

BELOW If your living room must double as a work space, it doesn't have to look like an office. Re-cover a functional chair in upholstery fabric, use a simple table as a desk, and store papers in a cupboard rather than a filing cabinet.

RIGHT The glass door of this armoire has been backed with a large-scale flower print that complements the more delicate pattern on the purple curtains.

THIS PAGE Don't be afraid to mix fabrics from different eras. Two contrasting 20th-century styles blend in this converted industrial space, where vintage floral cushions sit comfortably on a streamlined sofa. The monochrome print curtains tone with the upholstery and are clipped to an unfussy tension wire that doesn't take attention away from the large window.

ABOVE A crisp, lightweight piece of cotton fabric printed with bold squares of muted color makes an eyecatching cloth for an occasional table in a neutral environment.

ABOVE RIGHT In a sparsely furnished, high-ceilinged room, where the visual focus is on the low-level furniture, fabric panels casually draped over seat-backs convey the right informal note.

OPPOSITE Books really do furnish a room, and here the geometric structure of the built-in shelving is echoed by the swirling 1970s-inspired prints used for the pillow covers.

Wallpaper goes in and out of fashion—giant laser-print enlargements of a single image are currently much in vogue—but a good rule of thumb is to team patterned walls with plain furnishings or vice versa.

Plain white or colorwashed walls, combined with a neutral carpet, woven matting, or bare floorboards, are the perfect foil for old fabrics. If you are planning a room from scratch, it is simpler to pick a paint for

the walls that tones with your chosen fabrics rather than trying to find a fabric that matches an ideal color: you can easily get latex specially mixed to a particular shade.

Careful planning and use of pattern and color can make a small room seem bigger, or a large room even more spacious. For a dramatic effect, you can mix and match patterns on different scales, or combine stripes with florals or geometrics with plains to show them to best advantage.

Not everybody can, or wants to, buy completely new furniture to harmonize with a new decorating scheme: most of us live with an accumulation of items that have been inherited, passed on by friends

moving to smaller homes, acquired years ago—or even found in dumpsters by the squirrels among us. Adapting what you already have is all part of the fun, and can spark new and innovative ways of using things.

Comfortable seating where you can sit back and relax is the most important feature in any living space so, if you are going to buy just one item, make it a good sofa or large armchairs. Remember, too, that the sofa is usually the dominant (and most expensive)

piece of furniture in the room, so choose one that you will be happy to live with for some time. A small living area doesn't necessarily need a tiny sofa: play with scale, and you will find that an oversized two-seater or two-and-a-half-seater can increase the feeling of space and make a positive statement.

Unless you are going for leather or a buttonback chesterfield or chaise longue, slipcovers are always preferable to upholstery. They can be washed as necessary, and you can even have two

OPPOSITE Bright colors have a strong impact in neutral settings. The fuchsia and violet shades of these luxuriously fringed velvet pillows look even more vibrant against pale slipcovers and a cream wall.

ABOVE The hexagonal patchwork, fringed throw, and crocheted pillows lend this plain sofa a welcoming air. The effect would be far more cluttered if they were set against patterned covers.

ABOVE RIGHT A simple antique chair stripped back to its natural wood is a good foil for a striped woven fabric. Brass upholstery nails form rows of shiny spots that break up the monotony of the straight lines.

By putting traditional elements into a new environment—and placing a few carefully chosen vintage pieces against a modern backdrop—you can bring a classic mood into your living room.

sets one made in light fabric for summer and the other in heavier, darker cloth for the winter. Seating cushions can be replaced if they have become a little lumpy, but if the only problem with your existing sofa is cosmetic—that is, you simply don't like the look of it any more—it can be temporarily disguised under layers of fabric. A large cotton sheet or old candlewick bedcover, tucked well in, can be layered with wool blankets, throws, and quilts.

At one time, no sofa or living-room chair was complete without a set of antimacassars, also known as "tidies". These lace-edged cotton rectangles covered the back of the seat to prevent the upholstery from being stained by macassar oil (the shiny hair pomade worn by some men). Antimacassars were introduced at the beginning of the 19th century, when powdered wigs fell out of favor and fashionable men smoothed down their hair instead. Up until the advent of Brylcreem, decorative antimacassars were to be found in virtually every parlor, but they are almost obsolete today. Armcovers, often matching, were another practical and useful accessory.

Interior design cliché it may be, but a clutch of bright pillows, artfully scattered around a room, introduces a splash of color and visual focus to otherwise plain surroundings. Welcomingly plumped-up, they simply invite you to sit down, curl up, and relax with a magazine or good book.

When it comes to pillows, you can go for anything from a coordinating set in matching prints to an ad hoc mixture in assorted sizes made from good pieces of old fabric and trimmed with tassels, fringe,

ABOVE RIGHT A clutch of individually designed pillows in mismatched antique fabrics draw attention to the oatmeal sofa without detracting from the magnificent architectural features of this elegant room.

RIGHT A heavily stuffed, bewhiskered cat covered in pink-striped mattress ticking has found a useful role as a quirky door stop.

or braid. The square or rectangular form of a pillow cover has always provided an ideal opportunity for some deft needlework—just big enough to complete without getting bored—and there are plenty of surviving antique examples in an enormous variety of textile media.

Berlin woolwork pattern charts depicting an array of flower garlands, cabbage roses, posies, spaniels, sleepy cats, men on horseback, biblical scenes—and even portraits of Robbie Burns or Lord Byron—were cross-stitched onto canvas by patient Victorian women, and are faithfully reproduced by manufacturers today. Their original makers would

LEFT This Scandinavian-style living room, decorated for the most part in just two colors, shows how well a limited palette can work when you are planning an interior scheme. A cream-painted settle and cupboard are adorned with red and white fabrics, reinforcing the overall color scheme. The wooden seat is made warm and welcoming with feather-filled cushions, and a panel of gingham fixed behind a glass cupboard door makes the room appear less formal than it might otherwise have been.

not recognize these modern imitations, however: the faded colors we see today were once vibrant, chemically dyed yarns in alarmingly vivid shades of cerise, chrome yellow, bright purple, and lime green. Under the yellow tinge of gaslight or candlelight, they would have appeared much more muted.

Not until the introduction of electric home lighting were paler colors used in interiors, for fabric furnishings as well as walls. In the early 20th century, patchwork cushions, particularly hexagonal ones, were made during long winter evenings, and transfer embroideries on linen were popular in the 1930s. Even the once-derided Afghan crochet square is being revived on a tide of 1970s design nostalgia.

Making your own pillow covers is an ideal way to use up smaller pieces of fabric or to re-use the best areas from a quilt, curtain, or garment that is worn beyond use. Knitwear, too, can be recycled, in keeping with the current trend among interior designers to use wool throws and natural textures. Arran jumpers or indigo cotton knits with cabled patterns can quickly be transformed into covers if you cut off the arms, trim the front and back into two matching rectangles, and seam them together—use the flexible stitch recommended by your sewing-machine manufacturer for jersey or knitted fabrics. The patchwork wool cushion described on pages 40–41 takes this idea a stage further.

Professionals always finish off a cover with a zipper, but—since zippers can be tricky to insert—it is easier to sew the front and back together around three sides by machine, slip in the pad and close the fourth side by hand with slipstitch. This can be unpicked if the cover has to be dry cleaned or laundered. Alternatively, you can make the fastening into a feature using interesting buttons, ties, or

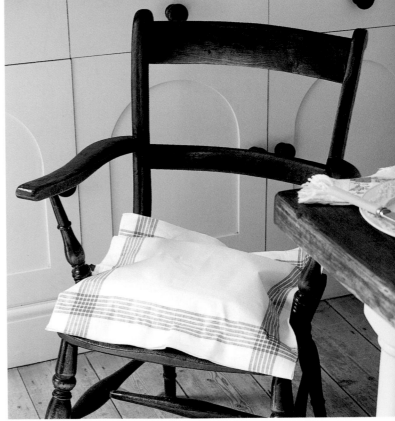

OPPOSITE, LEFT In this unpretentious setting of bare boards and exposed beams, traditionally upholstered seating would look out of place. Instead, the inhabitants have simply thrown a large white sheet over the long sofa and tucked it in. With the addition of a striped bolster and a plump square cushion, it strikes just the right informal note.

OPPOSITE, RIGHT A simple linen napkin, placed over a cushion, makes this country kitchen armchair a more comfortable place to sit.

RIGHT Rag-rug making was at one time a skillful and highly valued craft that utilized leftover fabrics and the parts of outworn garments that could not be cut down and re-made or turned into patchwork. These were cut into narrow strips and woven into a canvas background with a special hook. This brightly colored 19th-century example looks wonderful on the quarry-tiled floor of a country kitchen.

Making pillow covers is an ideal way to re-use parts of a quilt, curtain, or garment that has seen better days.

ribbons. Bolsters—padded, cylindrical cushions—are often used on sofas and daybeds. You can make almost instant covers for them by hemming the two short sides of a strip of fabric, then joining the other two sides to make a tube. Push the pad into the center, then gather up and tie the loose fabric at each end with a length of ribbon or cord, just like a Christmas present.

After the seating, the window treatment is the second most important feature in a living room. Since it is often the largest space in a house, the living room is likely to have the largest windows—perhaps a three-sided bay at the front in 19th-century buildings, or a large picture window overlooking the yard in more modern homes. Think about the design of your windows, and whether you want to make it into a feature. An understated treatment will emphasize the shape of elegantly proportioned sashes or leaded casements, and thick frames can be camouflaged with gathered panels of billowing voile.

Most of us have moved on from the elaborate, Victorian-style curtains—complete with swags, tails, and holdbacks—that were so beloved and widely copied by interior designers in the 1980s. These kind of window dressings are expensive and, unless your room is of stately proportions, can be overbearing. The modern approach is much simpler, with a bigger emphasis on the fabric itself than on the way it has been made up. This is especially the case with vintage textiles, where the material you are using may well be unique.

Do not underestimate the damaging effects of sunlight on cloth. If you are re-using old curtains, you may find that the lining has become brittle after years of hanging at the window; these should be replaced to extend the life of the main cloth, and antique fabrics will need the extra protection of a cotton lining when being made for the first time.

The prospect of calculating drops, seam allowances, and matching repeats is enough to discourage most people from sewing their own curtains or shades, but there are lots of instant alternatives that involve minimal stitching—and which are suited to one-off lengths of fabric.

One of my favorite solutions is to use decorative metal clips to attach a simple hemmed panel to a tension wire. In a similar vein, a café curtain heading—consisting of a simple channel sewn along the top edge—eliminates the need for complicated heading tape. Pieces of ribbon and loops of tape or lace can be used to make bows and tabs to hang a curtain from wooden rings or directly onto a rod.

When the curtains or shades you want to use in your living room are not conventional, the solution may be multilayered window treatments. If you have set your heart on a beautiful but impractical fabric — maybe an old sari that filters the light beautifully but doesn't block it out—you can team it with a functional blackout roll-up shade. Made from plasticized white fabric, these are unobtrusive during the day and are especially useful in rooms where maintaining privacy is important.

If you can find them, original Nottingham-style net curtains, machine woven from thick cotton, still look stylish, although they are much heavier than the sheers that now most frequently perform the task of screening windows from outside view. Most of the designs are floral, but among the pictorial devices are the ubiquitous crinoline lady from the interwar

ABOVE Dogs are not the only ones who appreciate their creature comforts. A folded vintage quilt immediately transforms this deep windowsill into an inviting window seat. The cushion cover has been fastened with pairs of tape ties in such a way that the inner pad gently bulges through the opening, adding to its plump and luxurious feel.

RIGHT Country does not have to mean folksy—apply urban minimalism to a rustic house to achieve a serene look. The walls and beams in this entrance hall have been painted white, and the traditional umbrella stand replaced by a giant log basket lined with vintage ticking.

patchwork woolen pillow

Anybody who has ever accidentally put their favorite piece of knitwear in with the week's laundry will know exactly what machine washing can do to pure wool. The fibers shrink and clump together, creating a thick, feltlike fabric— with the result that your treasured sweater can be worn by no one larger than a small child. Textile artist Lattika Jain puts this effect to creative use and scours thrift shops for sweaters and cardigans to recycle into wonderful household items. This patchwork pillow cover is made from a selection of muted stripes, fair isle knits, and toning plaid, backed with bright red corduroy.

materials and equipment

selection of old 80– 100% woolens and wool fabrics

corduroy shirt

decorative button

matching sewing thread

sewing machine

sewing kit

18in (46cm) pillow form

small safety pin

preparing the wool

Wash the sweaters in a hot wash and tumble dry. Iron with a pressing cloth to remove any creases.

cutting out

front panel

sixteen 5in (12.5cm) squares of wool

back panel

one 18in (46cm) square cut from the back of the corduroy shirt

ties

four 1 x 9in (2.5 x 23cm) strips of corduroy

facing

two 2 x 18in (5 x 46cm) strips of corduroy

1 Set the wool squares out in four rows of four, taking time to get a balanced arrangement of pattern and color. If you wish, you can join three 5in (12.5cm) long strips together to make a pieced square.

2 Pin and baste the squares together in vertical rows, overlapping the edges by ¼in (5mm) to get a flat seam. Set the machine to the stitch recommended for stretch fabrics and sew together. Join the four rows in the same way to make a square.

3 If the shirt has pockets, you can unpick one of them and sew it to the center of the back panel, adding a decorative button to fasten the top edge in place.

4 Pin and baste the front and back panels together around the sides and bottom with right sides facing. Machine stitch ½in (1cm) from the edge. Clip the bottom corners and turn right side out. Ease the corners into shape and press lightly.

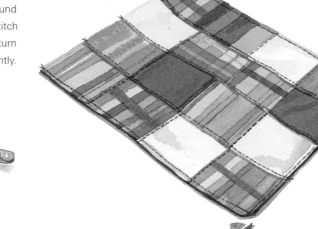

5 To make the ties, fold the strips of corduroy in half widthwise with right sides together. Pin, baste, and machine stitch close to the edge, then attach a safety pin to one end. Pass the pin back through the tube to turn it right side out. Fold under one open end and stitch across to finish.

6 Press under and stitch a narrow hem along one long edge of both facings. Pin and baste two ties to the right side of each strip 5in (12cm) from the short ends, matching the raw edges. With right sides together, join the short ends with a ½in (1cm) seam and press the seams open.

7 Slip the facing over the top of the cover, matching the seams and raw edges. Pin and baste together, then machine stitch along each side, ½in (1cm) in from the raw edge. Fold the facing to the inside, and topstitch to reinforce the opening.

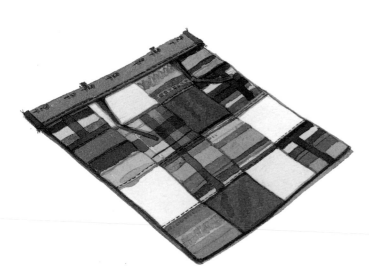

8 Pin the front and back together along the facing edge, 3 in (8cm) in from each corner, leaving an opening in the middle. Baste, then machine stitch close to the edge. Slip the pillow form inside the cover through the opening and knot the ties together to close.

BELOW A new take on an old patchwork technique, this innovative Cathedral Window pillow is beautifully made from plain and embroidered cotton and linen. This is a wonderful way to give a new lease on life to all those tray cloths and napkins that have already spent several generations hidden away in drawers.

RIGHT The appeal of this country living room lies in the restrained use of pattern and bright color. It enhances the original woodwork while increasing the sense of space within the room. The sofa is covered with a huge patchwork quilt and stacked with a variety of stitched, tapestry, and vintage fabric pillows. Even the chessboard has been carefully placed to echo the square border around the quilt, and the letters on the log cupboard add a lively finishing touch.

If you aim to combine the best of the old and the new in a contemporary setting, modern period charm and vintage style can be achieved without becoming mere pastiche.

ABOVE Roman shades are a neat and unfussy way to dress windows—the billowing fabric of conventional curtains would be overpowering in this particular room. When pulled up, the shade forms a series of neat horizontal pleats and reveals the frame, making it the ideal minimal window treatment. The use of a bold red-and-white checked fabric perfectly suits the geometric lines of the shade.

years, country scenes, windmills, ducks and even hot-air balloons. It is unwise to cut down a lace panel—not only does this ruin its value, but also you may wish, at some time in the future, to hang it at a larger window. Instead, try gathering it to fit the space or doubling over the top edge.

To achieve a fresher effect, plain voile curtains can be trimmed along the bottom or leading edge with bobble fringe or antique lace so that they have extra weight and will fall in soft folds. A clean, ironed sheet, with the turnback folded to the front to make a self-valance, makes an impressive lightweight curtain for a tall sash window or French doors.

Window dressings can be further ornamented with improvised valances and tiebacks—and this is an area in which you can really use your imagination. Borders of deep crochet edging cut from old tablecloths or narrow cotton runners can be gathered onto curtain wire and fixed above the window to make valances, and anything from an old necklace to a scarf, belt, or silk tie can be fastened to a wall hook and made into a holdback.

There are other uses for curtains in your living space. Before the widespread introduction of central heating, portières, or door curtains, were often used to keep out drafts, and they also make good room dividers as an alternative to folding doors, or screens to conceal televisions, videos, DVDs, and CD players, containers for tapes, and other intrusive black boxes.

If you have pieces of fabric that are too small or too precious to put at the window, they can be hung from the walls, either tapestry-style from poles—a long-established decorating technique that was used in Roman villas—or mounted over artists' stretcher frames as pictures in their own right.

Traditional gathered and pleated silk lampshades have acquired a rather fusty image, but vintage fabrics and trimmings can be used in a much more straightforward way to make contemporary covers for ceiling and table lights.

Making a new lampshade can be as simple as sticking bead fringe around the bottom edge of a ready-made cardboard shade or covering it with textured material—but for a really stunning effect, you can revamp old metal-framed shades (they often turn up in thrift stores and at yard sales). Strip off the original coverings, including any tape around the struts, and you will be left with a wire skeleton. This can then be bound from top to bottom with ribbon or lace, hung with loops of colored glass beads to refract the light, or strung with fake pearls. Take care to use a low-watt bulb so your creation doesn't burst into flames!

ABOVE Edging the gracefully proportioned windows of a townhouse, this window seat is padded with a long rectangle of upholstery foam, covered in delicious pink and soft cream fabrics. The different-sized pillows continue and expand this color scheme to create a stylish, feminine effect.

ABOVE RIGHT The dark, neutral-colored upholstery of this large sofa prevents it from dominating the room, but huge shiny pillows in rose pink and bright scarlet—each decorated with a band of printed fabric—bring it to life and pick up the colors of the nearby lampshade.

OPPOSITE, LEFT AND RIGHT Desirably tactile pillow covers have been made by mixing a range of textures, from wool blankets to fake fur. Less can mean more—and the neutral colors used in these covers look as effective on a 20th-century classic as they do on the wooden chairs (left).

Lack of storage is a constant problem for most of us, and space is often at a premium. Objects just seem to multiply of their own accord so that shelves and cabinets fill up with a profusion of books, papers, files, ornaments, high-tech equipment, and (for those of us with small children) toys. In our living rooms especially, this can be a problem: there are many items that need to be kept on hand but which don't always look interesting or attractive enough to have on show.

When all the existing space has been filled, try to utilize the "hidden space" in a room. You can use some of your favorite fabrics to cover hat and shoe boxes, for example. They make elegant storage containers, which can remain on show, stacked inside an empty fireplace, under a table, or on a high shelf.

And if you just can't stand to be parted from your remnant collection, button box, and ragbag, make a feature of them by displaying neatly folded fabrics and jars of beads in open wicker baskets for everyone else to play with and enjoy.

sleeping

Your bedroom is the most personal space in your home, so it should be a calm sanctuary from the outside world. This is the one room where you can indulge your dreams and feel at peace with the world, so make it truly your own. To create a tranquil atmosphere that is conducive to love, rest, and relaxation, surround yourself with your favorite objects and the muted colors of beautiful fabrics.

If you share your bedroom with a partner, you may have to confront the eternal style dilemma: whether your decorative scheme should be based on girly opulence or cool minimalism. For example, while you may yearn for a chi-chi boudoir, your partner would rather be in an industrial loft space that doubles as a study or gym (or vice versa).

The combination of traditional and contemporary style that lies at the heart of vintage chic provides a good compromise, bringing together an up-to-date sensibility with the best of a rather more elegant age—and the result doesn't have to be fussy, overtly feminine, or floral.

Linens, silks, chiffons, and chintzes from different eras can be mixed and matched harmoniously with old or new furniture—but, to be truly effective, they

ABOVE Giant squares of assorted fabrics were used to make this duvet, which is specially shaped to fit around the bedposts. Similar patchwork could quickly be made from the large swatches in sample books.

OPPOSITE, LEFT Roses are a perennial favorite in the home just as much as they are in the garden. A selection of printed fabrics and accessories such as this bag can be jumbled together for a riot of blooms.

OPPOSITE, RIGHT In a reworking of an old favorite, wool hot-water bottle covers have been recycled from knitted sweaters and are just perfect for snuggling up to on a cold winter's night.

need to be set off against a plain backdrop. Unless patterns have a "breathing space" around them, the room they are in will tend to look overfull. You will find that basic white walls, ceiling, and paintwork—on architectural features such as window frames, doors, baseboard, fireplaces, and moldings—do not appear as stark as you might expect, particularly if you choose one of the subtle shades of white that are widely available.

Textures are as important as colors in a room, if not more so, and by assembling an assortment of solid-colored antique fabrics, curtains, and bedclothes in similar or harmonizing shades, you can play different surfaces off against each other. Sheer voile curtains and smooth cotton sheets mixed with a luxurious satin eiderdown and deep-pile velvet cushions give movement and visual interest that will enrich your surroundings.

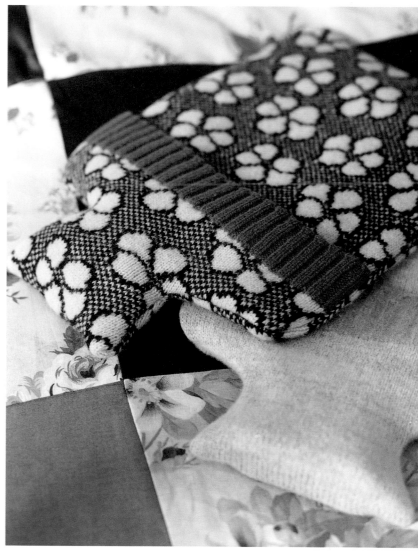

Many of the antique fabrics and accessories that survive today have done so against the odds, which only adds to their fascination value. Pillow shams, candlewick bedspreads, and counterpanes have gone in and out of fashion in the same way as clothing and shoes, and day-to-day items have always been discarded when they become outworn or outmoded.

Especially in the case of older artefacts, often only the best and sentimentally valuable items were kept—for example, appliqué

damask duvet cover

A set of monogrammed napkins discovered in a Paris flea market was my starting point for this patchwork. The red borders had faded to dusty pink, which combines well with the soft lilac, blue, and white of the other damasks. The cover is backed with an antique sheet and tied with tape bows. When choosing the fabrics, look for details, such as laundry marks and makers' labels, that can be re-used and stitched onto the cover.

materials and equipment

selection of laundered damask napkins
  and tablecloths
white cotton double sheet
100in (2.5m) woven tape
matching sewing thread
dressmaker's pins
sewing machine
sewing kit

cutting out

The instructions are for a double-sized duvet cover. Adjust the measurements accordingly to fit a larger or smaller duvet. Cut the back panel and facing from the sheet so the existing hems lie along one short edge of the back panel and one long edge of the facing strip.

back panel

width = 80in (200cm)
length = 92in (230cm)

facing

width = 2in (5cm)
length = 80in (200cm)

1 To make the front panel, trim off the hems and cut away any damaged areas from the napkins and tablecloths to give a selection of strips and rectangles in different sizes. Lay the fabric out on the floor in an approximate 88in (220cm) square, taking time to get a good balance of shape and color within the arrangement.

2 Start by sewing the smaller pieces together, then join them to form larger blocks, until the front is complete: pin and baste each seam, then stitch ½in (1cm) from the edge. Press the seam allowance to one side and topstitch ⅛in (3mm) from the seam. Trim the finished panel to 79in (200cm) square.

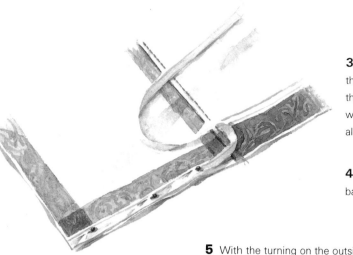

3 Pin and baste the facing strip along the bottom of the front panel so that the right side of the strip is against the wrong side of the panel. Stitch together along the bottom edge, ½in (1cm) from the edge, then press the facing to the right side. Pin in place, stitch along the same edge, ¼in (5mm) from the seam, then topstitch the edge of the facing to the cover.

4 Press 12in (30cm) along the hemmed edge of the back panel to the wrong side, making a deep turning.

5 With the turning on the outside and right sides together, pin and baste the top and sides of the front and back panel together. Machine stitch ¼in (5mm) from the edge, then trim and finish the seam allowance with a zigzag or overlocking stitch. Turn right side out and press.

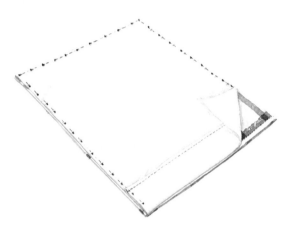

6 Pin and baste the front and back panels together for 10in (25cm) on each of the opening and machine stitch close to the edges.

7 Mark the positions of the ties by placing five pins at regular intervals along both edges of the opening.

8 Cut the tape into ten 10in (25cm) lengths. Finish one end of each tie, then press under a narrow hem at the other end. Baste, then handstitch each tie securely in place on the inside of the cover.

in half lengthwise, join the selvedges to form a new seam, and re-hem the sides. This way, the useful life of expensive linen and cotton could be extended for several more years before it was cut down for crib sheets and, eventually, dustcloths.

Fine lace-edged pillowcases and sheets may come at a premium, but a market is growing for mixed bales of linens that are now exported from central and eastern Europe. The best of these are laundered and, through dealers, find their way into specialized outlets. They can usually be identified by the stitched turnbacks, messages, and monograms, and the use of blue, buttercup-yellow, and turkey-red embroidery threads.

Look out also for old cotton lace or lengths of white crochet edging, and use them to trim your own plain sheets and pillowcases. (There always seems to be a lot of crochet edging about. It may be that people simply enjoyed making it and never got around to sewing it onto anything, although it was often unpicked and re-used when a tablecloth or runner became outworn.) You may wish to add embroidered initials to sheets and pillowcases in traditional style.

If you prefer the comfort of a duvet to sheets and blankets, you can make a cover from washable fabrics—dyed or plain sheeting, large squares of dress

ABOVE A group of Venetian looking glasses, along with a mirrored box and frame, sit happily beside a whimsical crocheted hat and a sequined floral panel in the corner of a chic bedroom.

OPPOSITE, LEFT Bedroom furniture from the 1920s, such as this oval-mirrored dressing table, originally had a dark and gloomy wood finish. But it becomes cool and elegant when painted. The flowered curtains and pashmina draped over the stool add to the room's feminine ambience.

OPPOSITE, RIGHT Sumptuous silk and velvet flowers—essential accessories for couture dresses in the 19th century—were assembled by hand in tiny Paris ateliers. Vintage examples are much treasured, but they are still made, and can be found in speciality ribbon and trimming shops.

and patchwork quilts, beribboned nightgown bags and the best Egyptian cotton sheets.

Antique bedlinen that has been washed and ironed for a couple of generations acquires a special sheen and an appealing softness which encourages a good night's sleep. But it is not always easy to find bedlinen in good condition, and the best lace-trimmed linen can be expensive.

You may come across an old sheet that has been carefully patched or turned "sides to middle." When the center part became worn and thin, frugal housewives would cut the sheet

Flowers have a classic appeal that transcends the constantly shifting trends in interiors and fashion. Choose old and new floral prints, embroideries, and accessories to create a look that can be added to over the years and which will not date.

RIGHT The random selection of colors and patterns used in this large-scale patchwork adds to its charm, giving it a fresh, uncontrived feel.

BELOW RIGHT If you want to send a romantic message to somebody special, order traditional woven nametapes from a specialized supplier with your own personal wording.

OPPOSITE A stack of antique eiderdowns worthy of *The Princess and the Pea* shows how easily the subtle shades of diverse geometric, floral, and paisley prints blend together.

prints, cotton scarves, and bandanas would all work well. I used a selection of damask napkins and tablecloths for the patchwork cover described on pages 48–49.

Old eiderdowns are much sought for their faded sateen or rose-and-paisley-patterned covers. Once thought of as purely utilitarian and covered with counterpanes, they are now put on show on top of the bed. Old eiderdowns can be drycleaned—but, if you are wary of the idea of old feather fillings or find them a bit musty, there are new ones around. Some of these are made in India and France, others by fabric and accessory designers such as Londoner Cath Kidston who specialize in contemporary versions of whimsically nostalgic kitsch and classic prints.

Antique patchwork, appliqué, and wholecloth quilts—usually thought of as the classic period bedcovering—remain eternally

ABOVE Too pretty to put away but too fragile to wear, this glamorous 1930s chiffon tea dress is displayed against the bedroom wall on a matching padded hanger.

LEFT A chintz remnant has been set under the glass top of this dressing table. It is complemented by a padded jewelry box in a similar print.

OPPOSITE, LEFT Old-fashioned feather-filled eiderdowns and quilts, piled high, add texture and softness to a bedroom.

OPPOSITE, RIGHT Checked, striped, floral, and paisley fabrics have been stitched together in a simple patchwork pattern to make a feminine bag to hold nighttime essentials.

popular. New versions are being made in both traditional and contemporary designs as part of an unbroken tradition.

Although many manufacturers produce new lines of fabric specially designed for patchwork—some of it reproduced from old prints—the quintessential character of patchwork springs from the practical element of recycling and re-using.

For centuries, scraps and remnants of fabric have been pieced together to make new designs, layered with batting, and stitched together, and there is a tradition of quilting in many countries. It was in the U.S., however, that the creation of patchwork quilts became a genuine art form.

The first European settlers took their fabrics and frames with them across the Atlantic and made quilted curtains, petticoats, and bedcovers for warmth. As a result, the earliest American quilts echoed English and Dutch tastes. Broiderie perse—where motifs cut from patterned chintz were appliquéd onto a plain background—was especially popular, and before the weaving industry was established, when all fabrics were imported, it was one of the only ways to create a fresh design. By the 1850s, however, there was a new creative confidence. This led to a flowering of intricate appliqué designs

handkerchief curtain

The children's printed hankies used to make this hand-stitched curtain date from the 1960s, when boxed sets of seven, each labeled with a day of the week, were popular gifts from grandmothers and aunts keen to encourage neatness. They feature a quirky variety of designs, ranging from nursery-rhyme illustrations and classic Mabel Lucie Attwell pixies to bears in helicopters and contemporary cartoon characters: Bugs Bunny, Tweety Pie, and Sylvester. For an adult's room, you could collect ladies' handkerchiefs decorated with embroidery or edged with lace.

materials and equipment

selection of printed
  handkerchiefs
white bias binding
rickrack
narrow gingham ribbon
decorative buttons
matching sewing thread
sewing kit

1 Wash and press the handkerchiefs, then lay them out on the floor to match the size and shape of the window, allowing an extra 6in (15cm) across the width to create a little fullness when the curtain is hung.

2 Line up whole handkerchiefs along the bottom edge, then trim others to size as necessary to give a straight top.

3 Slipstitch them together (see page 120), passing the needle through the existing hems to give an invisible seam. Join in vertical blocks, then sew the blocks together.

4 With right sides together, pin and baste one edge of the bias binding to the curtain top along the crease. Fold it over the raw edge, baste and machine stitch down.

5 Pin, baste, and hand-stitch a length of rickrack over the binding.

6 For the ties, fold a 12in (30cm) length of ribbon in half and stitch it to the back of the bias binding at each seam and at the two corners.

7 Trim the ends in fish-tails and sew a button to the top edge at the base of the tie. Press, then hang at the window.

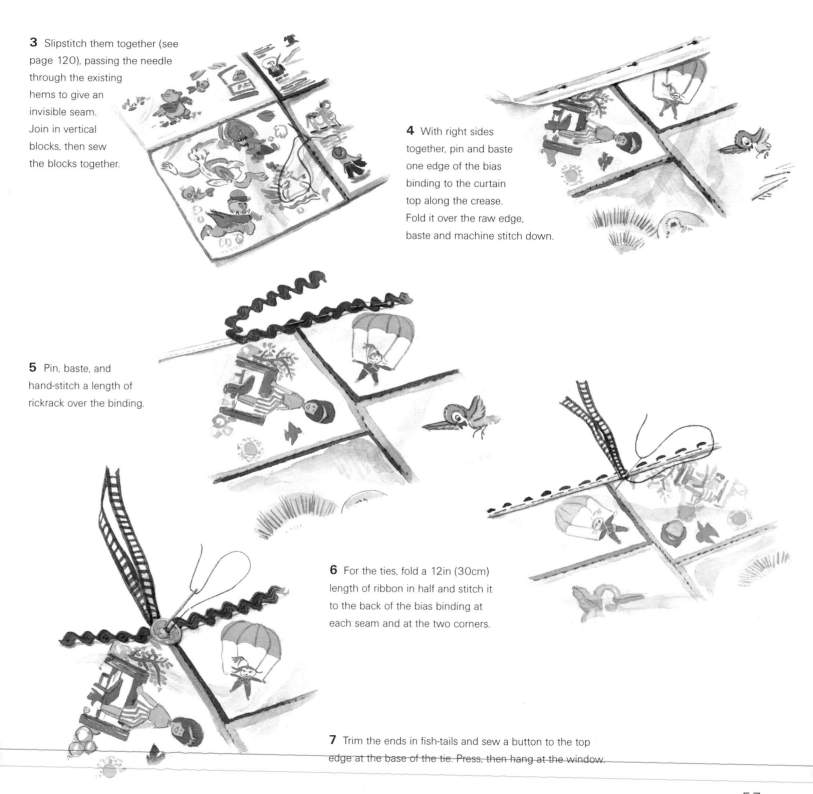

and geometric patchwork based on repeated square patterns, whose names reflected their makers' life and experience in a pioneer nation: Log Cabin, Bear's Paw, Moon over the Mountain, Tippecanoe, Rocky Road to Kansas, and Road to California.

Each quilt, whatever its source, can tell its own history, and the fabric used to make it often belonged to different members of the same household. Look carefully and you can often pick out pieces cut from flowered print dresses, embroidered baby clothes, or striped working shirts. Victorian soldiers made flannel patchwork from scraps of uniform fabric, and during the Depression years, resourceful American women used the printed sacks in which their animal feed was delivered to make blouses, aprons, and, of course, patchwork.

Old quilts should be treasured and cared for well. Although they may have been washed many times in the past, the hand-stitched threads that hold them together become fragile with time

BELOW LEFT A crisp gathered ruffle gives the finishing touch to a glazed chintz eiderdown made from a sprigged print of buds and open roses.

BELOW RIGHT The smallest details often have the most impact: the narrow white lace border around the edge of this pillowcase perfectly offsets the formality of the stripes.

OPPOSITE Even the humblest net shopping bag can be given a new lease on life. Here an assortment of bags containing everyday items has been hung from a chest of drawers to maximize storage space.

Sheer voile curtains and smooth cotton sheets mixed with a satin eiderdown and deep-pile velvet pillows give visual interest that will enrich your surroundings.

BELOW Shades don't have to have complicated strings, rings, and pleats. This straightforward rectangular panel hangs from three hooks and can be looped up during the day to let in the light.

and can break under the strain of being spun in a modern washing machine (a process that can damage cotton batting). Dyes may fade with new detergents, and dry-cleaning is far too harsh. The best way to revive and freshen a musty quilt is to lay it on top of a clean sheet in fresh air and sunlight for a few hours. Ingrained dirt can be removed with a vacuum cleaner: tie a piece of gauze over the head used for upholstery using a rubber band and gently run it over the quilt. You will be surprised at how much dust and grit comes out.

In the same way that a sofa tends to dominate a living room, the bed is bound to be the most important piece of furniture in the room where you sleep. Antique bedsteads with brass or wrought-iron frames look magnificent and make a focal point in a fashionably bare or a well-filled room. With a comfortable sprung mattress (rather than the original horsehair and feather combination), they appeal to the nesting instinct in us all. Antique bedsteads do, however, tend to be somewhat narrower than new beds—so, if you prefer more space, the best solution may be to choose a new bed and dress it with vintage fabrics. A four-poster or half-tester style will provide ample opportunities for romantic drapes and hangings.

ABOVE Where possible, display your favorite textiles rather than storing them out of sight. The bed is the perfect place to exhibit a precious quilt and a collection of vintage cushions and pillows.

RIGHT In a light and airy country bedroom, a multi-layered window treatment of patterned translucent voiles and boldly checked curtain fabric on a chunky wooden pole is both versatile and functional.

LEFT A brooch cushion is a good way to show off your jewelry collection and looks wonderful on the dressing table. This one is made from two heart-shaped pieces of toile de Jouy and filled with batting—add a handful of lavender or dried petals to give a gentle fragrance as you pin on the brooches.

OPPOSITE, LEFT An all-white color scheme has been chosen for a period bedroom. Textile touches—the lace parasol under the table and the faded rose pillow—enhance the dreamy atmosphere.

OPPOSITE, RIGHT This romantic bedroom is set in the gabled eaves of an old house. The antique bedstead is decked with vintage pillows, and the gathered fabric lampshades perfectly complement their brass urn bases.

Carefully chosen vintage textiles bridge the traditional and modern to give old and new bedrooms a timeless quality.

Period bedroom furniture ranges from a matching Edwardian set—including armoire, washstand, cheval mirror, and chest of drawers—to the most basic nightstand, originally intended to hold a chamberpot, and a Thonet bentwood chair. The classic curved dressing table with its triple mirror was to be found in most homes during the mid-20th century. The framework for this was often a very basic structure with shelves and drawers, but it was concealed behind a pretty gathered skirt.

Armoires for the wealthy were magnificent affairs with mirrored doors, plentiful hanging space, specially labeled shelves, and cedar-lined drawers to deter moths. Cottages and artisan houses often had a built-in cupboard beside the chimneybreast for clothes. This recess could be turned into a makeshift storage space by putting a pole inside the alcove and hanging a curtain across the front.

When it comes to decorating your bedroom, don't forget to look inside your closet for ideas. Take inspiration from vintage and contemporary clothing and display your favorite accessories, jewelry, scarves, or frocks. Even the most outrageous catwalk trends eventually filter down to home furnishings: embroidery, paisley prints, and beadwork can be found in the most fashionable homes, as well as on the best-dressed people.

OPPOSITE Storage space always seems to be at a premium in a child's bedroom, so open shelving such as this, set within an alcove, is extremely useful. It can be used to display textiles as well as for clothing and toys.

BELOW In the age-old tradition of "make do and mend," this tiny blue jacket has been cut down from an adult garment. The reverse seams (with the raw edges on the outside) and the hand stitching give it immense contemporary appeal.

RIGHT An appliqué denim-clad cowboy and his lassoo-twirling cowgirl partner constitute the decorative motifs on two versatile storage bags. The fabric has been skillfully chosen to give the pair an authentically Wild West appearance.

children's rooms

The scaled-down world of childhood inspires creativity—perhaps because we all long to recapture the exuberance of our own early years. So drop your preconceptions and let your imagination run wild in discovering the pleasures of decorating a child's room or baby's nursery.

Like any bedroom, a child's room should have a comfortable, calm atmosphere. Children enjoy having a personal space, where they can relax in their chosen surroundings. Left to their own devices, most children would end up with pink feathers, pop idol posters, and pile upon pile of clothes—no doubt you will have to compromise your own taste to meet their wishes somewhere along the line.

Children's likes and dislikes change rapidly, so plain walls and a bare wooden floor make an adaptable starting point to which, over the years, you can add or take away curtains, blinds, rugs, throws, quilts, big floor cushions, and beanbags. The shabby chic of a vintage look is a good informal alternative to the coordinated sugary pastels and cartoon characters available in chain stores.

The present generation of parents are not the first to be faced with an onslaught of themed merchandise aimed at children—as early as 1901, the writer Beatrix Potter endorsed Peter Rabbit slippers. The first dressmaking and upholstery fabrics designed especially for young people appeared at about the same time. These featured anthropomorphic animals, nursery rhymes, pixies, alphabets, and Kate Greenaway-style prints of sweet little girls in pinafores. Understandably, surviving examples are rare, but they can sometimes be found and given a contemporary twist with florals, ginghams, or deckchair stripes. Vintage nursery curtains look wonderful, but as an alternative, smaller pieces of fabric can be sewn onto ready-made panels to make a border or all-over pattern (use a blackout lining to encourage longer sleeping hours).

There are many other ways in which you can adapt old fabrics to new uses for babies and children. It is quick and easy to customize a ready-made cotton cover for a basket with appliqué flowers or to trim a receiving blanket with eyelet lace. If you like the idea of doing some patchwork but don't fancy spending several years making a regular bedcover, a crib quilt is the perfect-sized project. Soft old cotton sheets can be used to make pillowcases or cut down and hemmed

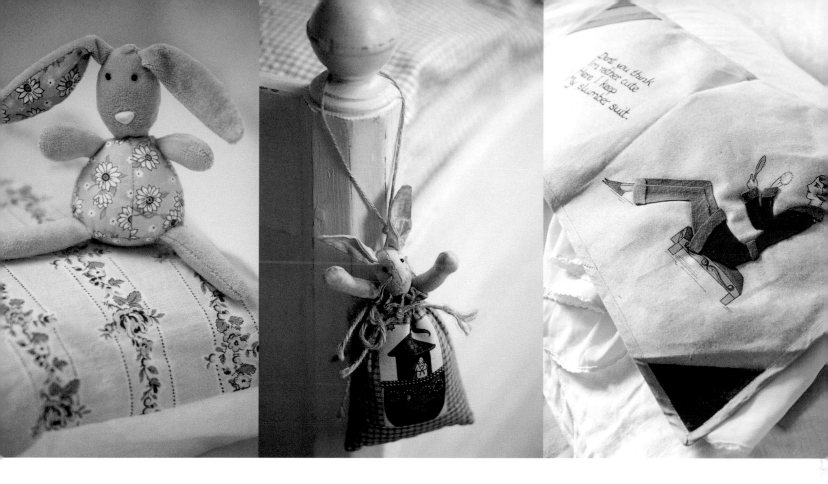

to fit small beds. You could edge the turnback with cotton lace and, in European tradition, embroider a reassuring bedtime message such as "sweet dreams" or "sleep well, my little angel."

Children are natural hoarders, and most parents have experienced the temporary irritation of having their home taken over by children's books, bright plastic toys, and primary colors, as well as countless shoes and pieces of clothing. Adaptable storage is the only way to stem the tide. If storage space is limited, transform your remnants of upholstery fabrics into big drawstring bags and hang them from pegs or hooks. A large circle of fabric with a drawstring channel around the edge makes a good playmat: the ties can then be pulled up around the toys to make a bag, without having to clear them up first.

Even your smallest pieces of fabric can find a use—together with your children, you can have hours of enjoyment making rag books, dolls' dresses, scarves for teddy, and curtains for the dolls' house. But, as all children know, the best thing to do with old clothes and lengths of material is to pul them on—so fill a dressing-up box with all your castoffs and spare finds to provide the props for endless games of make-believe.

OPPOSITE, ABOVE A row of knitted and cloth bears sit happily together on a shelf. The smallest one is made from a pink-and-green cotton print—if you long for your own flowered bear, hunt down a toy pattern book and simply substitute a vintage floral for fur fabric.

OPPOSITE, BELOW Twin beds in an attic bedroom have been dressed with matching covers and accessorized with matching chairs at the foot. A small bag slung from the bedpost acts as a child-sized pajama case.

ABOVE LEFT The rabbit's body is made from a ditsy daisy print. A similar toy can be made with fabric from a child's outgrown dress or blouse.

ABOVE CENTER A Noah's ark bag with a simple drawstring provides a good home for another rabbit. Basic appliqué like this is quick to do—use iron-on bonding web if you don't feel like lots of stitching.

ABOVE A 1920s-style flapper in a slumber suit adds a touch of chic to a traditional envelope-shaped nightgown case.

baby quilt

This blue and white album quilt was made to celebrate the arrival of my son Alexander and has his name and date of birth embroidered along one edge. Following an Irish custom that a young baby should be wrapped in garments belonging to its relatives to bring good fortune, I incorporated scraps of shirting, embroidery, and dress fabrics collected from members of our close family. The patchwork blocks are all based on traditional "four-patch" designs, some of which have evocative names—Puss-in-the-corner, Whirligig, Windblown Square, and Batchelor's Puzzle.

materials and equipment

selection of white, solid, and
*   patterned cottons*
embroidered cotton fabric
old linen or cotton sheet or
*   tablecloth for backing*
natural cotton batting
matching sewing thread
white quilting thread
quilting needle
sewing machine
sewing kit
thin cardboard
paper glue

cutting out

finished size: approximately
*   43in (110cm) square*

quilt top

thirteen patchwork blocks
twelve squares of embroidered
*   cotton, each 8½in (23cm)*

filling

47in (120cm) square of cotton
*   wadding*

backing

47in (120cm) square
*   of sheeting or linen*

border

four strips of blue cotton, each
*   3½ x 47in (9 x 120cm)*

making the patchwork blocks

Each of the thirteen blocks consists of sixteen individual squares, some of them made up from two triangles. Draw two templates to the measurements shown below, glue them onto thin cardboard, and cut out. A seam allowance (a) of ¼in (6mm) is included, and the dotted lines represent the sewing lines. All the blocks are assembled in the same way, apart from the Variable Star squares (see step 6).

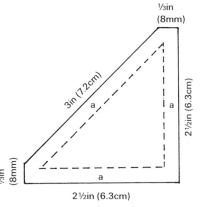
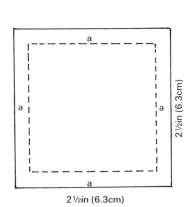

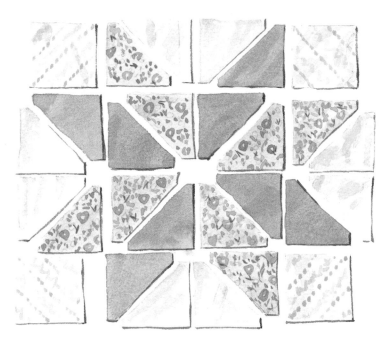

1 Draw around the templates on the fabric using a dressmaker's pen and cut out around the outlines. Following the pattern (left), make the squares and triangles needed for the first block and lay them out on your work surface.

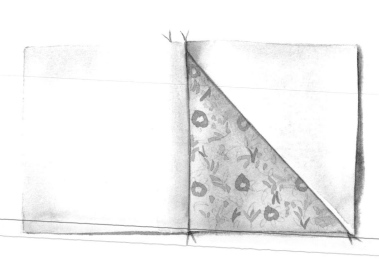

2 Pin and baste the pairs of triangles together along the diagonals and machine stitch ¼in (6mm) from the edge. Press the seam allowance towards the darker fabric.

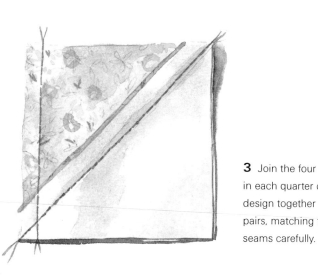

3 Join the four squares in each quarter of the design together in two pairs, matching the seams carefully.

4 Press the seam allowance, then sew the rectangles along the long edges to make four larger squares.

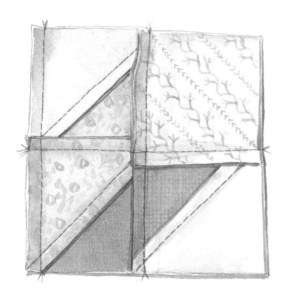

5 Stitch the four quarters together in pairs to make two rectangles; press and join along the center seam to complete the block.

6 For the center of the Variable Star, cut an 4 1/2in (11.5cm) square. Join the two squares at each side of the center in pairs, then sew them to the large square. Sew the top and bottom rows of four squares together to make long strips. Stitch the three pieces together to complete the block.

7 To assemble the quilt top, arrange the patchwork blocks and plain squares in a checkerboard pattern. Sew together in five strips, then join the strips, matching the seams carefully.

8 Lay the backing fabric right side down on the floor and place the batting on top. Spread the quilt top centrally over the batting, right side up. Baste the three layers together with basting thread, stitching from the center out to the four corners, then to the middle of each side. Sew further parallel lines of basting stitch, 8in (20cm) apart, to cover the whole surface. Baste around the outside edge of the quilt top.

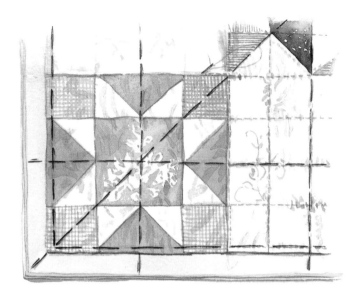

9 To quilt the plain squares, draw a 2in (5cm) grid across each one with a dressmaker's pen and ruler, in line with the blocks on each side. Using a quilting needle and quilting thread, work a round of short running stitches ⅛in (3mm) inside the edge of the square, then stitch along each line. If you would like to do more stitching, you can then outline each of the white patches and the centers of the blocks. Trim the batting and backing, leaving a margin of 1in (2.5cm) around the edges of the quilt top.

10 Embroider a date and name along one border strip if you wish. Press each of the four strips in half lengthwise, then press under a ¼in (6mm) turning along each long raw edge. Open out and, with right sides together, pin and baste the first strip along one edge of the quilt, so that one edge lines up with the edge of the quilt top and there is an overlap of 1in (2.5cm) at each end. Machine stitch along the crease nearest the edge, through all three layers, leaving 1in (2.5cm) unstitched at each end. Repeat with the other strips and press.

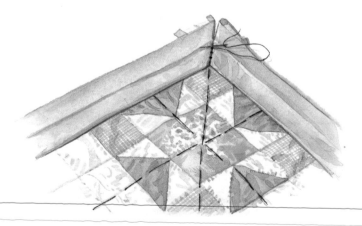

11 To miter the corners, press the end of each strip under at a 45-degree angle, and slipstitch the seams as far as the central crease. Trim the seam allowance to ¼in (5mm).

12 Fold the strips to the back of the quilt. Miter the corners as for the front, trimming away the surplus fabric. Pin and baste the border in place, then slipstitch the turned-up edge to the quilt. Finally, take out all the basting.

LEFT Pan-handle covers are among those small essential items that can enhance any kitchen. This one was made from an old sweater that had been felted—see the project on pages 40–41 for how to do this.

BELOW Just because oven gloves are functional doesn't mean that they can't also look attractive. Like the handle cover, this glove with a metal eyelet hanger has been made from felted wool and trimmed with a flower-print cuff.

OPPOSITE Everything goes in cycles. No longer dismissed as the decade that style forgot, the 1970s are trendy again, and the bright geometrics that characterized the era are once again to be found in the most fashionable kitchens.

cooking & eating

Old fabrics help to create a warm and welcoming ambience in a kitchen, the traditional heart of the home. Whether you favor minimalism, kitsch, or country style, there are plenty of vintage kitchen textiles that are still practical for daily use.

Tablecloths and napkins, known collectively as "napery" from the French word *nape* (tablecloth), are easily found because they were produced in such vast quantities. Cloths specifically for kitchen use come in every guise: candy stripes, ginghams, naturalistic and stylized fruit and flowers, and novelty prints—all of which echo the upholstery and dressmaking fabrics of their time. In mid-20th-century America, housewives favored pictorial or floral patterns with a center panel and deep borders. These are highly sought after, particularly those with a state theme such as leisure activities in the Garden State of New Jersey, palm trees in California, and folk art in Pennsylvania. For the obsessive collector, the goal is a full set representing all 51 states.

Elsewhere, Willow Pattern designs were made to match the kitchen china, and on a similar theme, a blue-and-white-checked cloth combined with coordinating striped Cornish ware has a jolly air, suited to a country or contemporary kitchen. The most practical kitchen table covers were washable oilcloth, thin, plastic or vinyl. Not many originals have survived, but there are nostalgic reproductions on the market that work well with older fabrics.

Patterned cloths were, and are still, used every day for breakfast and lunch, but for elegant dining you may want something more formal. By unfurling a crisp white cloth across your table

apron

This 1970s-style apron conjures up memories of happy childhood afternoons spent watching my mother baking and stirring the cake mixture with a huge wooden spoon. Designer Emily Medley has mixed floral and geometric prints in a yellow, brown, and orange color scheme, and the apron is reversible—so, in true retro-entertaining style, you can match your apron to your outfit!

materials and equipment

main cotton fabric

contrast cotton fabric

matching sewing thread

sewing machine

sewing kit

cutting out

apron

For the front, cut a 33 x 40in (85 x 100cm) rectangle from the main fabric. Fold in half lengthwise with right sides together. Pin along the top and half of the side edges. Mark a point on the top 11in (28cm) in from the corners and a second point on the sides 12in (30cm) down. Draw a curve to join the points. Pin

just inside the line, then cut along it. Cut the back the same size from the contrasting fabric.

pockets

From the main fabric, cut a 10 x 20in (25 x 50cm) rectangle. Fold in half widthwise and draw a curve across one corner. Pin both layers together just inside the curve, then cut out. Cut another pocket from the contrasting fabric to the same shape.

from the contrasting print cut:

tabs

two 2 x 6in (4cm x 15cm) strips

ties

two 2½ x 36in (6 x 92cm) strips

neck loop

6 x 24in (60cm) strip

appliqué

Cut out two life-sized wooden-spoon shapes from the contrasting print.

1 Pin and baste the two "spoons" to the front of the apron, one on each side, 8in (20cm) from the top. Set the machine to zigzag and sew around the edges.

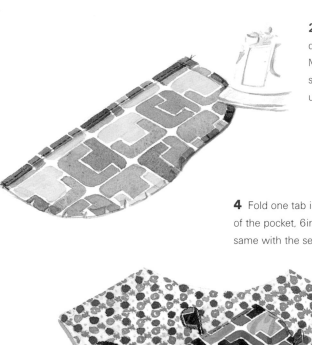

2 Fold under and press a ⅔in (2cm) double hem along the top of each pocket. Machine stitch close to the inner fold. Cut small notches along the curves, then press under ⅔in (2cm) around the raw edges.

3 To make the tabs, press each strip in half lenthwise with wrong sides together, then press a ½in (1cm) hem along each long edge and refold. Pin and baste the edges together, then work a row of machine stitch ⅛in (3mm) in from each side.

4 Fold one tab into a loop and baste to the wrong side of the pocket, 6in (15cm) from the right corner. Do the same with the second tab on the other pocket.

5 Pin and baste the first pocket to the front, covering the ends of the spoons, and machine stitch close to the edge. Work a second line of stitches ½in (1cm) further in. Sew the second pocket to the back in the same way.

6 Make the neck loop and ties as for the tabs, pressing under one short end of each tie to finish. Pin and baste the neck loop to the right side of the front, ½in (1cm) in from the top corners, raw edges together. Pin and baste the open ends of the ties in place ½in (1cm) down from the bottom of the curve, raw edges together.

7 With right sides together and the neck loop and ties drawn into the middle, pin and baste the front and back together, leaving the bottom edge open. Clip the corners, then turn right side out and press. Press under a 1in (2cm) hem around the open edge, then pin, baste, and machine stitch the edge together.

and laying it with the best flatware, china, and glass, you can set the stage for a memorable evening.

White linen and damask napery has always been used for special occasions, and large tablecloths with eight or more matching napkins were often given as wedding presents or bought as part of a dowry. Old sets may be passed down through families, but a collection of non-matching napkins is quick to assemble and can look just as effective.

Damask is double-sided jacquard cloth, with an integral design—usually a decorative edging with an all-over pattern of scrolled leaves, cherubs, flowers, or fruit—woven into the fabric. Twining strands of ivy are often found and, since they represent "marriage bonds" in symbolism associated with plants, sets with this design may have been wedding gifts. Look out especially for embroidered initials and entwined monograms, worked in white thread or to match a colored border. Often these were dowry linen: legend has it that a girl would work her own initial in her youth and add that of her husband once she was betrothed.

Like many other aspects of social behavior, rigid etiquette once applied to using napkins. In past centuries, diners were expected to tuck a corner of the napkin into their collars, much as we do with small children today, to protect fine clothing from splashes and

spills. This signaled appreciation of good food, and dinner napkins were therefore very large. As late as 1951, the Good Housekeeping Institute advised that: "Full-sized dinner napkins are at least 24in square, luncheon napkins about 18in square and the smaller, more elaborate serviettes used at tea-time are about 12in square." Fortunately, we are now more relaxed, and most guests don't mind very much if their table linen is not the correct size.

Napkin folding is a quirky craft that has recently been revived. Mrs. Beeton provided step-by-step diagrams for a "water lily" or "mitre" to hold a bread roll, a "fleur-de-lys" to sit in a wine glass, and the simply frivolous "slipper" to sit on a side plate. These origamilike fabrications are easy to reproduce using a well-starched napkin. For a less formal setting, simply fold napkins in half and roll

OPPOSITE This country table cover was once a bedspread. Hexagonal patchwork is most effective when fabrics are put together randomly—see page 123 for how to do this.

ABOVE LEFT A dove-gray and white ticking tablecloth is a good foil for the muted blue of the antique Asiatic Pheasant earthenware plate and bowl.

ABOVE Glass-fronted hutch doors have been backed with blue-striped fabric—but the kitchen china inside is too attractive to hide away totally.

RIGHT Even tiny scraps can be put to new use. This curtain is made from pieces of blue and white fabric and lace, and hung from ribbon loops.

RIGHT Looking for all the world like pixies' hats, and ready to enliven the breakfast table, these conical egg cozies are made from quarter-circles cut from an old wool sweater and seamed along the straight edges.

BELOW A staircase separates the food preparation area of this balcony kitchen from the living area, where a sofa with a braid-trimmed red-and-white-checked slipcover and vintage pillows provides a good place to sit and chat to the cook.

them up, then tie a length of tape, lace, or ribbon around the center. Improvised napkin rings can also be made from beads threaded onto shirring elastic and strips of fabric fastened with interesting buttons.

Special rituals always accompanied the custom of taking afternoon tea. Bone china cups and saucers were brought out, along with the smallest napkins, a crochet-trimmed cloth, doilies for the cake plates, and, to keep the pot warm, that quintessential symbol of domestic gentility, the tea cozy. You can still find dainty squares of linen, edged with drawn-thread work or hand-embroidered with bows, floral motifs, and Victorian ladies. Different designs can be sewn together to make a tablecloth or kitchen curtain.

To go with the crinolined ladies in their country gardens, what better than a thatched cottage? Needlepoint tea cozies in the shape of half-timbered houses were fashionable from the 1920s on, and once I even found one that represented Charles Dickens's Old Curiosity Shop. Since they were not washable, they were kept for best. For everyday, striped wool cozies were popular.

THIS PAGE To make the under-sink curtain, hem the sides and bottom of the fabric and sew a ½in (1cm) double hem along the top. Pass a sprung curtain wire inside the fold and attach a screw eye to each end. Screw cup hooks into the work surface and hang the curtain in place.

Even if you are not the greatest cook, your takeouts
are bound to taste better in beautiful surroundings.

ABOVE LEFT Pretty towels and cloths hung from
rods add decorative touches to a country kitchen.

ABOVE RIGHT If your kitchen is tiny, think laterally
and use your hidden space: a net shopper is ideal
for storing pan lids.

Kitchens are lived-in, hard-working rooms, full of steam and cooking aromas, so any fabric furnishings in a kitchen—curtains, shades, or chair covers must be washable. If you are looking for a suitable window treatment, café curtains are a proven solution. These gathered, half-length curtains hang from a stretched wire or a narrow metal pole (sprung versions that don't need to be screwed in place are available). Making them requires minimal sewing. You need a strip of fabric one and a half times the width of the window and about 5in (12cm) longer than the required depth. Finish the sides, then make a double hem along the top, wide enough to slip over the wire or pole. Put it in place, then turn up

the hem, making sure it just skims the windowsill to prevent it from becoming damp. The lower edge can be trimmed with heavy cotton or crocheted lace for a real period feel; this is also a useful way to lengthen a piece of material that is too short.

Remember that such curtains are not limited to windows. In the days before built-in units, a cheerful cotton print curtain would be hung below the old-fashioned ceramic sink and wooden draining board to conceal the jumbled objects stored underneath. These large ceramic sinks are once again in vogue, part of the move away from the somewhat clinical kitchen of the late 20th century. Even if you don't like the solid appearance of rows of low-level and

ABOVE LEFT Positioned directly above the sink, these cotton checked curtains are bound to get splashed when the dishes are being washed, so they were chosen to be washable and practical.

ABOVE An ordinary cafetière is made a little more special with this insulating wool jacket, which matches the egg cozies shown on page 78.

hard day's cooking, you could make a slipcover for it, or hide the upholstery under an old cotton throw or even a tablecloth. Padded stool seats can be covered with fabric, and cushions, tied onto the back struts, will soften the seats of wooden kitchen or dining chairs and are a good way of using smaller pieces of fabric. Some are made to fit exactly, but if your chairs are squarish, ordinary cushion pads will do; simply add sturdy tape or fabric ties at two of the corners. Mismatched chairs can be given unity by making cushions from the same fabric, or you can use different remnants on each cover for a matching set.

wall-mounted cabinets, food, dishes, pots, and pans have to be stored somewhere. A curtain can always be hung on a work surface or deep shelf, providing ample space for freestanding vegetable containers, crates for tins, and a wine rack. If you really don't want the modern world to intrude, you can hide the dishwasher, tumble dryer, and washing machine behind other curtains.

Old-fashioned armoires have chicken-wire insets in the doors, which can be backed with panels of fabric, ruched at top and bottom, to prevent the contents from getting dusty. This idea can be copied by removing the center section of a paneled cupboard door, replacing it with mesh, and hanging a curtain at the back of the frame.

Upholstered furniture should be kept to a minimum in the kitchen, but a bit of comfort is needed. If you have room for a sofa or armchair to sink into after a

OPPOSITE, LEFT Use pattern with restraint to keep your dining area looking uncluttered. Red-checked cushions and cloth make the table the main focus of attention in this conservatory, while plain roll-up shades relegate the windows to second place, providing a neutral background for the curved lines of the candelabra.

OPPOSITE, RIGHT A hand-crocheted cotton cover, weighted with bright glass beads, is a traditional way to protect milk in a pitcher. You can make a effective substitute by stitching beads around the edge of a small doily or a circle of fine voile.

RIGHT These placemats of red-and-white patchwork with thick padded fillings are a practical way to protect a table surface. Along with the pitcher cover and the tea glasses, they add touches of color to an otherwise plain setting.

The one essential fabric item for every cook is an apron. As with other kitchen textiles, old ones are avidly collected; the full-length pinafore of the Edwardian maid and the serviceable floral coveralls of the mid-20th century, or frilly half-aprons designed to be worn for serving rather than doing anything very messy. Originals in good condition are comparatively rare, but you can make your own from lengths of antique fabric, a patterned tablecloth, or even by stitching the best bits of old dishtowels together.

Dishtowels are humble but necessary items which manufacturers have often made deliberately bright and colorful to enliven the drudge of drying up. Those that survive have had hard wear—often

OPPOSITE, ABOVE Patchwork is not only for bedcovers. These curtains, made up of myriad small squares in many different designs, look quite at home at the kitchen window, surrounded by an eclectic assembly of antiques.

OPPOSITE, BELOW A mosaic of tiny fragments of fabric was sewn onto a plain background and edged with decorative stitchery to make this satin "crazy patchwork" tea-cosy.

RIGHT A square net edging with a floral design has been added to a wide band of linen to make a practical café curtain to screen this kitchen sink.

until they began to disintegrate, when they were consigned to being floorcloths. Striped and checked cotton towels with a loose weave were produced from the 1930s on. During World War II, they were the only fabrics freely available in Britain, so resourceful stitchers there utilized them to make bedcovers, curtains, and even children's clothes. A kitchen curtain made from dishtowel material (which can sometimes be bought by the length) still looks striking and individual today.

Printed dishtowels are good examples of domestic art, and like tablecloths, they are many and various in their design. Irish linen glass cloths have minimal patterning and feature jacquard lettering on their colored borders. Novelty prints range from kitchen themes— pans, teapots, recipes, apple varieties—to the illustrative graphics of the 1960s. In addition to cute kittens and seaside souvenirs, you may come across calendars, which could be hung on the wall one year and used the next, and advertisements, which were often promotional offers for long-standing household brand names. Washed and pressed, dishtowels can be displayed on a clothes horse or hung with wooden clothespins from an indoor clothesline.

Once you start looking, you will find many other items that can make good kitchen accessories, some of them traditional, others new interpretations of old ideas. Vintage shopping bags have great

appeal and come in all materials, shapes, and sizes. If you can't track down the originals (and few have survived in good condition), the brightly woven plastics and raffia or bead embroideries of the 1950s and 1960s are being reproduced.

If you have got enough space on your wall, put a curtain pole just below ceiling level and hang a collection of bags from butcher's hooks as a decorative way to store items that are not in daily use. The European custom of re-using muslin bags as an alternative to plastic shopping bags should be copied more widely; making a simple rectangular bag with sturdy handles is straightforward.

There is something very alluring about the idea of walking to the store with a Red Riding Hood wicker basket over your elbow, however impractical it may be. But old shopping baskets make

great storage containers for linen, table mats, or dishtowels and can be lined with fabric to prevent the contents from snagging. There are many variations of the basic theme, and several baskets would look good lined up on a high shelf.

Open shelves make good display areas for smaller finds and creations, too; a row of your favorite recipe books with protective jackets made from printed linen cloths, jars of homemade chutney and jelly with fabric covers like tiny mobcaps, or just your favorite drying cloths, neatly folded and stacked. To complete the look, the shelves can be edged with lengths of crocheted lace or strips of patterned fabric. Even the unassuming folded paper chain—a cut-out row of pennants, flowers, or tiny people holding hands—has been used in the past as a trim reminiscent of folk art.

LEFT The checkerboard floor is the central feature of this stylish red-and-white themed kitchen. Highlights of red have been picked up in the cupboard curtains and other furnishings—made not from ordinary upholstery fabric, but from utilitarian linen dishtowels, which introduce an unexpectedly informal element.

ABOVE Letters, bills, and other household paperwork can be kept in order in this kitchen "office." The drawer fronts and recipe books are covered with dishtowel fabric and gingham, with monograms adding the finishing touches.

OPPOSITE, LEFT A zigzag edging, cut from cheerful gingham, gives a crisp, neat finish to a shelf of home produce. The jars are topped with squares of cotton, tied in place around the lid.

OPPOSITE, RIGHT Ready for teatime, a padded tea cozy sits next to the teapot in front of a hutch packed with decorative china

laundering

Vintage fabrics have a useful role in the laundry room. They can be transformed into covers for ironing boards and hangers, adapted to make all kinds of clothes bags, or made into sachets. And if they are to survive as practical or decorative items elsewhere in the home, vintage fabrics themselves need careful laundering and storage.

OPPOSITE To make this endearing clothespin bag, wash a child's sweater on hot, then cut an opening across the chest and bind it with contrasting tape. Stitch the hem together and trim with the remaining tape. Slip a wooden coathanger inside.

RIGHT To give your laundry a subtle fragrance, and to make ironing more relaxing, use a special linen spray or sprinkle a few drops of lavender essential oil into the mister bottle.

LEFT Padded coathangers, trimmed with lace and bows, will protect your best dresses and give an air of old-fashioned elegance to your closet.

Clothing, curtains, table linen, and bedclothes made from cotton or linen can last for many years with the right treatment. White tablecloths, napkins, and sheets that appear to be in good condition but have a slightly dank aura can all go in the machine. Soak them briefly in nonbiological powder or very dilute bleach before washing on a warm setting. Tumble dry on a cool setting for a short while, taking out the load before it dries totally. Hang the linens on a washing line if you have one—sunlight acts as a natural whitener.

Lace, embroidery, wool, and lace curtains should be handwashed in soapflakes. Rinse the item well, then place it between two towels. Roll up lengthwise and twist to squeeze out the excess water, then dry flat. If your fabrics are valuable or especially fragile, seek professional advice before washing, and avoid harsh chemical

RIGHT Neatly folded bundles of clean linen can be stacked up in baskets, labeled, and tucked away under the bed for safe storage.

BELOW Lavender bags have been used for millennia to fragrance fabrics. The plant's name derives from the Latin word *lavanda* (things to be washed) and is the root of the word "laundry."

OPPOSITE, LEFT Drawstring laundry bags, threaded with ribbon or fabric ties, can be quickly run up from rectangular remnants.

OPPOSITE, CENTER The fresh scent of a pile of clean laundry is a reward for all the hard work involved in washing and ironing.

OPPOSITE, RIGHT To cover a hanger, first pad it with cotton wool, bound in place with thread, and wrap ribbon around the hook. Cut a wide strip of fabric to fit loosely over the hanger and press a narrow hem along each edge. Hand-stitch in place with the seam along the center top.

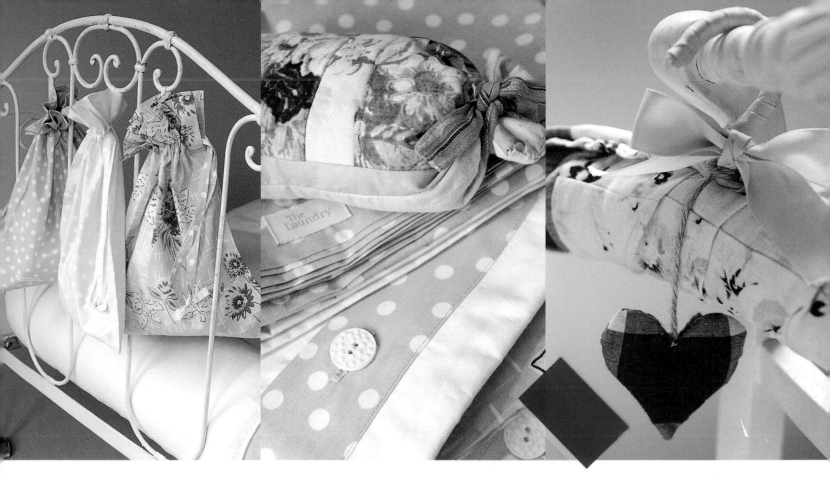

dry-cleaning. Detergents and stain removers can get rid of persistent mildew and rust marks, but they may fade old dyes. Test for color-fastness by wetting the back of a hem with detergent solution and blotting it with a tissue. If the dye runs, don't risk anything further.

Iron cotton and linen on the right side, along the length of the article, but iron lace curtains diagonally, or they will stretch out of shape. Fine materials should be protected by a pressing cloth and ironed on the wrong side. Place embroideries face down on a towel before ironing. Linens used to be starched heavily before storage, but the deep creases this produces can permanently mark fabric, so spray with starch only before the linens are used.

Relieve the everyday chore of ironing by using a length of vintage cotton to cover your ironing board. Remnants, old pillowcases, or even old huckaback towels can be turned into large drawstring bags to hold both clean and unwashed laundry. If you are really organized, you can make several, each labeled, so your weekly washing is sorted before you load it into the machine.

Fabrics that are not in frequent use should ideally be stored somewhere dark and dry. Linen "presses" were designed for this purpose and are roomy enough to hold a household's entire stock of linen. A chest of drawers or big cabinet is a good substitute: line the shelves or drawers with paper so the fabric doesn't come into contact with the wood. Wrap delicate fabrics in acid-free tissue and roll them to avoid straining the fibers. If you haven't got room to roll larger pieces, sandwich them between layers of tissue or gauze before folding.

Make sure long-term storage is not too warm in a centrally heated house. On a smaller scale, cardboard boxes are fine, provided they are not kept anywhere humid, but plastic boxes do not allow the air to circulate and can encourage mildew. To keep stored fabrics fresh, slip sachets of dried lavender between the folds. These are quick to make from scraps of lawn or voile. Alternatively, tie a handful of potpourri in an old lace handkerchief to make a scented bag to hang inside the linen cupboard door.

bathing

Bathrooms are full of hard and shiny surfaces—porcelain, chrome, mirrors, and enamel—which can make them appear chilly and unwelcoming. But with judicious use of fabrics and an eye for detail, you can turn even the most unpromising bathroom into a relaxing sanctuary. All those hard finishes can be softened with carefully chosen textile accessories, which will also add highlights of color and texture.

Tempting though it may be to install long curtains to break up an expanse of tiled wall, bathroom window treatments should be kept simple and washable (or wipeable). Venetian blinds are a well-tried solution, but rollup shades are easy to assemble from kits and can be customized. You can use almost any cotton or linen fabric if it is treated with a stiffening spray (available from good furniture suppliers and department stores). An old cotton net panel gathered onto a sprung wire or sheer organza or voile on tension wire will also screen the window effectively. Choose a fabric that is opaque enough to block the view at night when the room is brightly lit.

The shower curtain is likely to be the largest expanse of material in the room. Unless you go for a transparent, funky print, shower

stacked on open shelves. If you have the space to show them off, antique towels can be hung over a freestanding wooden towel rod or clothes horse. Made from textured cottons such as huckaback rather than the fluffy terrycloth we are used to, they are often bordered with bands of stitching and cotton crocheted lace.

In 1908, when colorfast embroidery threads were first on the market, *Fancy Needlework Illustrated* provided its British readers with flowing Art Nouveau designs to be worked in several colors

LEFT A shower curtain with a big splashy flower print in vintage style has been hung on a circular rail. Along with the patterned bathmat, it adds character to what would otherwise have been a purely functional period bathroom.

RIGHT This plain hand towel has been backed with a length of 1950s fabric that clashes gloriously with the wallpaper. It hangs from a different sort of rod—wooden spring clothespins have been glued to a length of painted wood and set close to the sink.

OPPOSITE, LEFT Lotions and potions can take up a great deal of space. Multipocketed storage like this, which can be hung from the door or wall, is a useful way to protect the bathroom from clutter.

OPPOSITE, RIGHT To save even more space, brushes and toiletries can be kept in long-handled bags tied to a hook on the back of the bathroom door. These felted versions are especially desirable.

curtains can be pretty drab, but they are easy to disguise. A hemmed panel of vintage material with eyelets punched along the top edge can be hung in tandem with a readymade curtain and draped outside the bathtub when in use.

Modern bathrooms tend to be compact, but those in older houses are often larger and may retain some original features—coving, a cast-iron fireplace, or a large reeded or frosted-glass window. A Lloyd loom chair piled with cotton- or terrycloth-covered pillows will provide a comfortable place to sit in a bigger bathroom. Neatly folded piles of towels look good of art silks and declared that: "Embroidered towels are a luxury of the age." Before then, only white, red, and blue threads had been permanent. The writer also recommended the use of linen towel shams — "serviceable items employed to cover towels which are in use and apt to look soiled, crumpled or untidy."

In addition to the washing pile and all those damp towels, bathrooms can easily become cluttered with the multitude of lotions, potions, jars, and sprays that we accumulate in our search for beauty and cleanliness. Some of these are attractive enough

to display, others are less so, but there are ways to get rid of the jumble. For example, you could try decanting shampoos and conditioners into glass bottles with ribbon bows or tassels tied at the neck. Other toiletries can be arranged in shallow wicker baskets that have been painted and lined with vintage fabric. Those that are not pretty enough to be displayed can be stored in simple drawstring bags, which can double as travel bags.

THIS PAGE Fluffy cream terrycloth bath mitts have been bordered with bands of fabric in a dusty rose print, which matches the other accessories in the bathroom and makes them just a little more special.

OPPOSITE, LEFT This is about as far from modern bathroom fixtures as you are likely to get—the rungs of a rustic ladder make a good alternative to a chrome rod for a selection of old cotton towels.

OPPOSITE, RIGHT While daylight is desirable in a bathroom, people using the room need to preserve their modesty, so any overlooked windows should be screened. Any fabric used in a steamy atmosphere needs to be easily washable, so this large linen cloth, used as a half-curtain, is a good solution.

This cool white bathroom with its vintage fitxtures is softened with faded curtains, a linen towel monogrammed in red, and a band of white lace around the sink, making it a perfect setting for the pink-flowered drawstring bag.

floral drawstring bag

Designer Caroline Zoob works from a studio in the English countryside, where she creates textiles that combine modern sensibility with a period style. She has an affinity with antique materials and made this drawstring bag from a 1930s fabric remnant. Her attention to detail is revealed in the narrow piping and contrasting edging, and the way each piece uses the floral pattern.

materials and equipment

antique fabric for the bag

white linen for the lining

16in (41cm) length of piping cord

two 20in (50cm) lengths of blind cord

matching sewing thread

sewing machine

sewing kit

small safety pin

cutting out

bag (antique fabric)

two 8 x 9in (20 x 22cm) rectangles

one 5½in (14cm) diameter circle for the base

1¼ x 16in (3 x 41cm) border strip

1¼ x 16in (3 x 41cm) bias strip cut with diagonal ends both sloping in the same direction (see page 120) for the piping

lining (white linen)

two 8 x 9in (20 x 22cm) rectangles

one 5½in (14cm) diameter circle for the base

1 Mark the position of the drawstring channel with two points on each long side of each bag rectangle, 1¾ and 2¼in (4.5 and 5.5cm) down from the top corners. With right sides together, pin and baste together and join the long sides with a ½in (1cm) seam, leaving the space between the marks unstitched. Press the seam open.

2 Join the short ends of the border strip, right sides together, with a ½in (1cm) seam. Press the seam open. With wrong sides together, fold and press the border in half along the long edge. Turn the bag right side out, then pin and baste the border around the top, matching the raw edges and the seam.

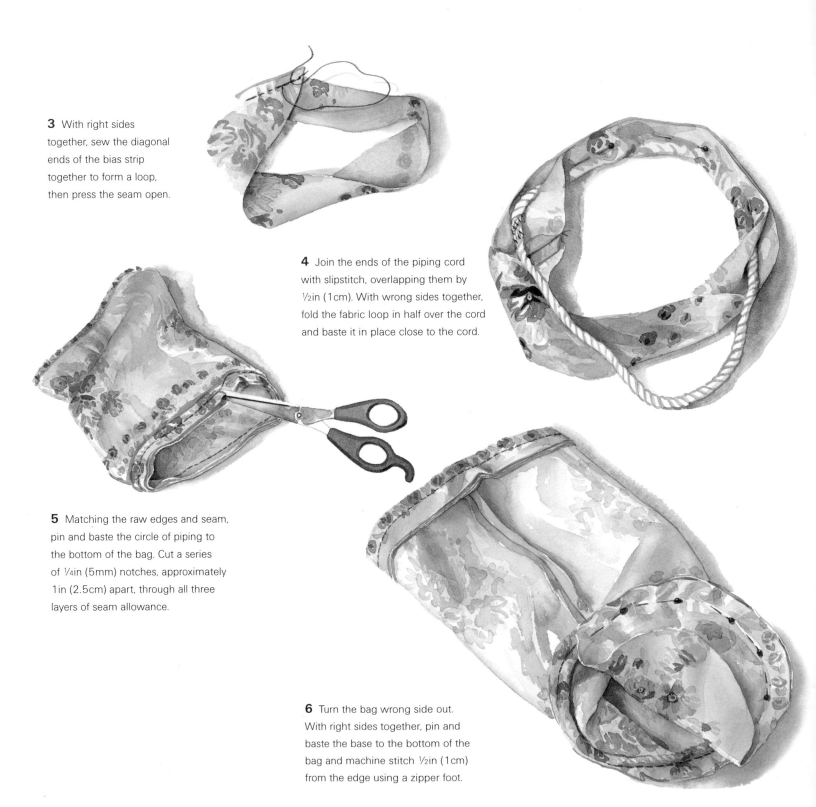

3 With right sides together, sew the diagonal ends of the bias strip together to form a loop, then press the seam open.

4 Join the ends of the piping cord with slipstitch, overlapping them by ½in (1cm). With wrong sides together, fold the fabric loop in half over the cord and baste it in place close to the cord.

5 Matching the raw edges and seam, pin and baste the circle of piping to the bottom of the bag. Cut a series of ¼in (5mm) notches, approximately 1in (2.5cm) apart, through all three layers of seam allowance.

6 Turn the bag wrong side out. With right sides together, pin and baste the base to the bottom of the bag and machine stitch ½in (1cm) from the edge using a zipper foot.

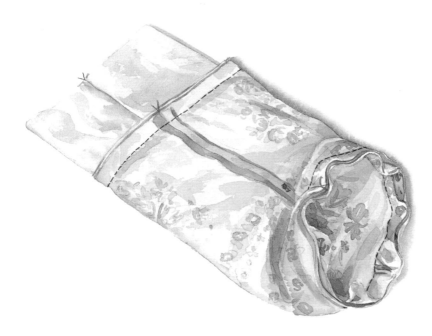

7 Pin and baste the two pieces of lining together, then machine stitch along the long sides ½in (1cm) from the edge. Leave a 2in (5cm) gap at the bottom of one seam for turning the bag right side out. Notch and join the base as in steps 5 and 6.

8 With right sides together, fit the lining inside the bag, matching the side seams. Pin and baste together around the top, then machine stitch, leaving an allowance of exactly ½in (just over 1cm).

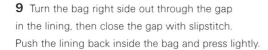

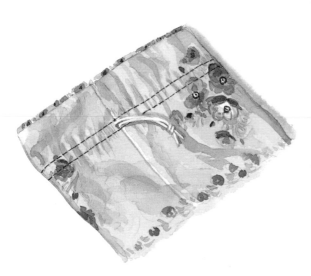

9 Turn the bag right side out through the gap in the lining, then close the gap with slipstitch. Push the lining back inside the bag and press lightly.

10 Rule two parallel lines with a dressmaker's pen to join the top and bottom of the gaps in the side seams on both front and back. Baste the two layers together between them. Work two rounds of machine stitch along the lines around the bag to form the drawstring channel.

11 Put a small safety pin at one end of a length of cord and thread it through one side of the channel, and out of the opposite opening. Knot the ends together and trim. Thread the other cord through the channel on the other side, then knot the ends and trim.

12 Cut a pentagon shape, approximately 2in (3cm) deep, from the remaining antique fabric, and press under a ¼in (5mm) hem all around. Fold in half over one of the knots, then baste in place. Slipstitch around the edges. Finish off the other cord the same way.

RIGHT The folding deckchair is a summer classic, found by the hundred in parks and on beaches, where the assorted stripes form a patchwork of color. If you prefer something more subtle, existing covers can easily be replaced with a strip of upholstery fabric, hemmed at the sides and nailed to the frame.

OPPOSITE, LEFT A checked tablecloth, draped over an antique garden table, sets the scene for dinner outside.

OPPOSITE, RIGHT The perfect way to enjoy a warm summer day is to take a comfortable chair out into the orchard, cover it with a length of vintage cloth—and sit back and relax.

outdoor living

Whether you are setting off into the wilds, spending a warm evening luxuriating on the beach, or enjoying the tranquility of your own backyard, outdoor living is one of the best ways to unwind. Even the tiniest backyard or balcony can be treated as another room, and by taking a few creature comforts outside, you can extend your living space into the open.

Nature's patterns and colors have provided endless inspiration for textile designers, giving us a rich legacy of fabrics that spans Indian palampores, hand-painted Chinese silks, William Morris furnishings, and Liberty dress cottons. Floral prints work as well outdoors as they do indoors. The overblown red and pink roses of a faded chintz are set off perfectly by green lawns, trees, and hedges, while the lavender and yellows of French Provençal prints conjure up memories of sun-soaked summer afternoons.

Living outdoors requires a less formal attitude than living indoors. The usual rules can be relaxed, and you can be bolder in your choice of color and pattern. Bright stripes or huge flowers that may be overwhelming in the living room look less obtrusive when they are surrounded by wider spaces.

Al fresco eating in the countryside or on a beach is a pleasure to be relished whenever the weather allows. A blanket on the bare ground is all you need for an impromptu picnic. Spread one over it and take a scattering of pillows along for real comfort. An old-fashioned hamper, equipped with plates, glasses, and flatware, along with a "real" tablecloth and napkins, is more ecologically sound than disposables, and lends to the atmosphere of a day out.

Garden furniture—wicker armchairs, sun loungers, deckchairs, wrought-iron chairs and tables—is essential for relaxing and dining at home. Purpose-made metal or hardwood furniture has

ABOVE LEFT If you are lucky enough to have a veranda, specially designed for open-air living, you will probably spend many evenings outdoors. The owners of this house have teamed director's chairs with a long table and equipped it with kerosene lamps for when the light fades.

ABOVE Garden benches can be very convivial if you have company, but big squashy pillows and a vintage rug are needed to make the wooden slats more comfortable.

OPPOSITE, ABOVE A canopy provides shelter from the heat of the day: the striped fabric used here complements that used for the pillows giving a bright, airy feel to a sunny balcony.

OPPOSITE, BELOW LEFT AND RIGHT A clapboarded veranda like this, with its subtly decorative fencing, needs minimal furnishing to preserve its clean lines. A potted plant provides a focal point, and a weather-worn bench with a faded cushion is all the seating needed.

the advantage that it can be left outdoors all year round, and the weathering effects of winter rain and cold only enhance its appearance. The somewhat solid seating can be softened by adding stacks of pillows, quilts, and throws. If space is limited, choose folding café chairs and director's chairs, which can be stored away when necessary.

If you want to be outside when the midday sun is beating down, you will need to create shade. Freestanding plastic canopies can be found in most garden centers, and they can be turned into inviting outdoor pavilions by draping them with lengths of fabric or, if you wish, making a tailored cover to fit over the frame. Sun umbrellas, windbreaks, and deckchairs can also be re-covered with ticking, checks, or flowered fabric to make them more individual and to suit your taste. As dusk falls, you'll be reluctant to leave this inviting space, but gas-powered heaters, garden candles, and solar-powered lamps will give warmth and light to extend the hours you can spend outside.

celebrating
& decorating

Causes for celebration among friends and families are endless: birthdays, Christmas, Easter, christenings, wedding anniversaries, good exam grades, new babies, moving home. Marking the occasion with a hand-made gift or by decorating your home will make it memorable, but by incorporating one-off pieces of fabric, lengths of lace, buttons, beads, and ribbons, you can make your presents and decorations totally unique—and you don't even need to be able to sew to create something special.

OPPOSITE This deceptively sophisticated Christmas angel is the sort of thing that becomes an heirloom, being taken out of storage every year to assume pride of place at the top of the tree. Festive tidings embroidered around the hem of her skirt make her really special.

RIGHT In some places, Christmas stockings are hung at the foot of the bed. To make sure that this one won't be overlooked, it has a message for Santa stitched along the top.

FAR RIGHT Garlands don't have to be made out of evergreen. This one is put together from looped galvanized wire and embellished with crystal flowers and beads from a chandelier.

christmas

Whatever the time of year, just thinking about Christmas is enough to unleash a flood of nostalgia for many a past holiday—as well as anticipation for the next one. Most of us have shared the excitement of a pile of enticingly wrapped presents, hoped for a last-minute fall of snow—and enjoyed plenty of good food, laughter, and companionship.

Each family circle or group of friends has its own distinctive way of celebrating Christmas, and different groups tend to establish over the years their own particular rituals and traditions associated with the festivities. The way in which a house is decorated at Christmas is an important part of the celebrations in that, by making it welcoming and attractive to family and visitors alike, you can create a warm atmosphere over the holiday.

Whether you are one of those people who cannot resist indulging in a Christmas extravaganza of Santas and sleighs, evergreen swags, festoons of paper chains, and cards on every surface, or if you are a minimalist at heart who would choose a few white-painted designer twigs in preference to a twinkling tree, it is worth considering a vintage approach to seasonal style.

LEFT Old-fashioned crocheted lace doilies can be hung from the tree to make contemporary snowflake ornaments.

ABOVE Tiny padded Christmas stockings to trim cards or use as gift tags can be made from the smallest pieces of fabric.

ABOVE RIGHT To introduce a change, try draping lengths of embroidery and crisp white lace over the branches of the tree instead of tinsel.

OPPOSITE, LEFT This blue plaid stocking has been cut from an old woolen lap rug

and cleverly incorporates the fringed edge to make a decorative cuff.

OPPOSITE, RIGHT These wonderful bead tassels date from the 1920s and originally came from the Paris workshop of couturier Charles Worth.

Antique fabrics and accessories will provide you with a muted palette and the richest variety of textures for your decorating scheme. The traditional combination of red, green, and white— inspired by berry-laden holly branches frosted with snow—has a classic quality that works well in faded shades. Plaids in these colors have an unmistakably festive air, and if you have wool blankets or lap rugs that spend most of their time in an old chest, this is the time to bring them out and use them as covers for guest beds or sofa throws.

Checked tablecloths and napkins are equally jolly and combine well with crisp white damask, sparkling glasses, and the best silver. If you want to add a little extra pattern, lengths of plaid

or striped ribbon can be used to edge plain linen or tied in bows around rolled-up napkins. Cotton crocheted mats, lace-edged doilies, and runners can be washed, starched, and used as the centerpiece for the dinner table. They show up well against a plain dark cloth.

In the mid-20th century, special sets of holiday table linen were produced, printed with designs featuring reindeer and sleighs, beaming Santa Claus figures, snow-covered trees, stars, and snowmen. These now have collectable kitsch appeal, and you may be lucky enough to come across an original.

Christmas decorations were often carefully wrapped in newspaper, placed in boxes, and stored away at the end of every December, so

a few antique items have managed to survive. Among the tinsel and tree lights, most families have a couple of very old painted glass balls or a venerable angel for the top of the tree, which come out year after year, and which have a charm all their own.

New decorations are frequently expensive and can look garish in comparison with the faded glitter and iridescence of old ornaments, but if you think laterally and improvise, you can find lots of vintage alternatives. Sort through the bead box and button tin for necklaces, tassels, sequins, fringe, and large crystal beads to hang from the branches.

Broad strips of fabric can be plaited to make garlands, rectangles seamed to make present sacks, and smaller pieces turned into Christmas stockings, while the tiniest scraps can be used to make gift bags and decorate cards or labels.

RIGHT Even the smallest fragments of lace can be pressed and mounted in a way that complements the delicacy of the fabric.

FAR RIGHT Romantic folk art motifs including hearts and birds have been incorporated into this satin patchwork picture, which was made to commemorate a wedding. If you want to embroider a message, write it directly onto the fabric using a fade-out pen, and sew over the line in backstitch or stem stitch.

gifts

In 1840, the author of a Victorian manual on needlework wrote somewhat sentimentally of "those numberless pretty and useful tokens of remembrance which, passing from friend to friend, soften our hearts by the feelings they convey." Today, personal handmade gifts are still exchanged in recognition of friendship and love. As much as in the 19th century, any present that has been specially made for the recipient is highly valued.

Whatever your level of sewing ability, there are many ways in which you can add a personal touch to the cards and presents you give. Fabric scraps can be stitched and embroidered to create greeting cards for Christmas, birthdays, Valentine's Day, or Mother's Day, but it looks just as effective if you simply cut out shapes and stick them onto a folded piece of heavy paper.

Fusible bonding web—available, with instructions, from fabric and craft stores—is useful for joining one piece of fabric to another for quick-fix gifts. Use this method to make instant appliqué on pillows or scarves, or for decorating a plain bag. All you have to do is trace your designs, cut them out, and iron them onto the background. Beads, buttons, and embroidery stitches can be added for extra interest.

MAIN PICTURE Look out for an old hardback edition of a friend's favorite novel and make a new jacket for it from flowered cotton fabric. Alternatively, you could buy and cover a thick bound notebook—or, for a New Year's present, a diary.

INSET This nautical card is made from three pieces of fabric glued to a rectangle of linen and mounted on a folded piece of watercolor paper. A few simple stitches add detail and character.

A gift or greeting card that has been made and decorated by hand is both precious and individual, and will always mean more to the recipient than something that was purchased readymade.

Small rectangles of fine cotton or organza may be used to make simple sachets that can be filled with dried lavender, rose petals, or potpourri and embellished with ribbon, lace, or other trimmings.

Larger pieces of material can be used to make protective covers for books. Try to find something that reflects the theme of the book—for example, a delicate sprigged voile for a romantic novel, a linen dishcloth for a cookbook, or a floral print for a gardening handbook.

If you have the time and skill to embroider an old-fashioned sampler for a friend's newborn baby or stitch an appliquéd picture to commemorate a marriage, your gift is bound to become an heirloom.

A crib quilt is another traditional baby present, but if you are reluctant to undertake the task single-handedly, think about making an album quilt as a group project. Each person sews a patchwork block, embroidered with their name or a message, which are then joined together to make the quilt top.

Sometimes you may find a vintage piece that is complete in itself, but which can be displayed to make a special gift. Three-dimensional items — kid gloves, beaded bags, mother-of-pearl or linen "washing" buttons on their original display cards — look good in box frames. Depending on your taste, embroidered motifs, doilies and pieces of lace

OPPOSITE Ribbon-tied bags can be made from fine lawn handkerchiefs or pieces of embroidered cotton. Fill them with lavender or dried rose petals to make fragrance sachets, or use them to wrap the smallest of presents.

LEFT These brightly colored brocade-lined bags, trimmed with braid and fringing, would make wonderful presents by themselves, but could also be used as containers for another gift to celebrate an important occasion.

BELOW Old beadwork may be too damaged to preserve in its original state, but it can be re-used. Unpick the beads and sequins and stick them onto polystyrene forms using short pins to make this luscious ball and Valentine heart.

edging can be displayed behind glass in ornate picture frames or mounted in simple clip frames.

Unusual presentation adds to the anticipation and excitement of receiving: think about how you can wrap a bought or homemade present to give it a really individual style. Rectangular remnants, fine handkerchiefs, or striped dishtowels can be made into simple bags or used to line a gift box or basket.

An ecologically sound alternative to using wrapping paper is to conceal a gift within a remnant of luxurious organza, an old silk scarf, or a starched napkin. You could even cut narrow strips of pretty prints to tie around a plain parcel instead of ribbon. For the finishing touch, make a hand-lettered gift tag and tie it to a length of narrow lace or cord.

weddings

Every wedding is unique, and, for each bride and groom, the occasion is a pledge of love, hope, and promise for the future. In diverse cultures across the world, couples mark their union with a blend of solemn ceremony and joyful festivity celebrated with family and friends. Countless old customs and superstitions surround weddings, all aimed at bringing good fortune to the new husband and wife as they embark on their new life together.

The tradition of the bride wearing "something old, something new, something borrowed, something blue" on her wedding day is widespread. It links her old family way of life to a new existence as a married woman, with the "borrowed" item symbolizing the present. Blue is the color that symbolizes the qualities of purity, loyalty, and fidelity (as in "true blue"). Vintage accessories not only fall into line with this romantic idea, but also have a elegance beyond changing fashion that will give a classic and timeless air to the celebrations.

Some weddings take place on the grandest of scales, in luxurious surroundings with dozens of guests. Others are more intimate occasions with just a handful of close friends, but however large or small the event, it can be made more personal with a few carefully chosen and individually made items. Wedding dresses have long

RIGHT AND OPPOSITE, ABOVE RIGHT Vintage clothing is once again in vogue among the fashionistas. This gorgeous cream wool gown with its densely embroidered edging of pearls and glass beads would be the dress of a lifetime for a winter wedding.

OPPOSITE, ABOVE LEFT The exchange of rings is a key point of any marriage ceremony, so make a ring pillow from textured fabric trimmed with the subtlest of edgings.

OPPOSITE, BELOW Instead of the usual box of rice, a cone of cardboard, covered in white fabric and edged with eyelet lace, can be filled with fresh rose petals.

BELOW LEFT AND RIGHT A shallow wicker basket is lined with antique fabric in gentle shades, trimmed with ribbon, and filled with cream roses. It could be carried by a bridesmaid or used as a table center for the wedding reception. Another idea for the reception is to tie handfuls of sugared almonds in small square napkins to make bonbonnières.

RIGHT An album covered with white linen will hold not just the wedding photographs, but all the other ephemera that have been accumulated by the bride and groom on the memorable day.

been trimmed with ruffles of lace or stitched with tiny beads—both themes that can easily be extended to decorating the special gifts and various accessories required for the bride, her attendants, the guests, and the reception venue.

Many brides wear a white or cream gown and a veil, although this is a comparatively recent convention. In the days when all garments were stitched by hand, few women could afford a dress that would be worn only once, and instead would get married in their Sunday best outfit. Antique veils are treasured as family heirlooms and may date back several generations. Sizes vary from shoulder- to full-length, and they have been worn in different ways, anchored with headbands, flower garlands, or tiaras, according to changing fashions. If you covet an old lace veil, but find it prohibitively expensive to acquire one, you can instead buy a length of fine silk net and stitch a length of cotton lace around the edge. The cheat's way to an instant vintage look is then to soak it in weak tea and rinse well before pressing.

Apart from the traditional bouquet or posy, the bride may also carry a good-luck token of some sort, often a four-leaf clover or horseshoe whose crescent shape, like the new moon, represents growth and fertility. A softly padded heart—the universal symbol of love—can easily be made from two heart-shaped pieces of

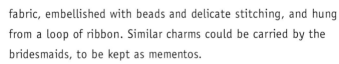

LEFT A wedding reception is the place to make your romantic dreams public and where you can be really indulgent. Make it equally memorable for the guests by dressing the tables with specially made covers, and bedeck them with antique beadwork and fresh flowers at each setting. This plain damask cloth is appliquéd with motifs that have been cut from floral upholstery fabric and machine stitched in place.

BELOW LEFT The sweetly named love-in-a-mist is the ideal choice for a wedding posy. Cover the stems with damp cotton and plastic wrap so the flowers will last, then bind them with broad lace.

fabric, embellished with beads and delicate stitching, and hung from a loop of ribbon. Similar charms could be carried by the bridesmaids, to be kept as mementos.

At the wedding reception, fresh flowers, white lace and beading will complement a classic tablecloth of crisp white damask. Give each place setting a handwritten name card and a handmade bonbonnière to make the guests feel genuinely special. Finally, instead of using shiny artificial ribbon, why not tie a band of eyelet or delicate bobbin lace around the wedding cake? Afterward it can be washed, starched, and stitched onto a small pillow, as a souvenir of a perfect day.

practicalities

You don't have to be a skilled needleworker to transform your vintage textiles. Some of your fabric finds will need only minimal alteration before they are put to new use—all you have to do is to cut them down to size or re-hem the edges—but if you want to make cushions, curtains, or any of the step-by-step projects, or do your own embroidery, the following illustrated instructions are here to guide you.

SEAMS AND HEMS

If you can hem the edges of a piece of fabric properly and join two lengths together, you have mastered the basic techniques of sewing and should be able to tackle most of the projects described in the earlier chapters.

PLAIN SEAM

With right sides together, line up the two raw edges and pin them at 2–4in (5–10cm) intervals. Use the parallel lines on the baseplate of your sewing machine as a guide to keep the seam allowance even. Baste, then machine stitch along the seam line. Take out the basting, then press the seam open or to one side (as directed).

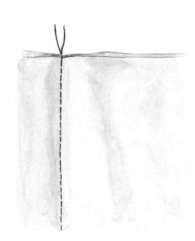

CURVED SEAM

The allowance on a curved seam has to be trimmed back to ⅓in (1cm) and clipped so the seam will lie flat. On an inside curve, make small notches. On an outside curve, snip a short distance into the allowance at regular intervals.

FINISHED EDGE

The cut edge of a plain seam may fray, especially if an item is washed, but this can be prevented by finishing the edge. If the seam is to be pressed open, work a line of zigzag or overlock stitch along each raw edge before seaming. If the seam is to be pressed to one side, the seam allowance can be trimmed and the two edges joined together with a zigzag (as shown).

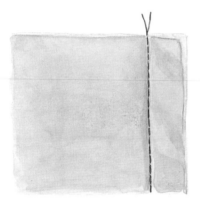
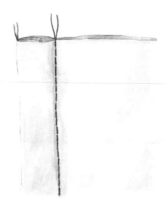

FRENCH SEAM

Used for joining lightweight or sheer fabrics, a french seam encloses the raw edges completely. With wrong sides together, stitch ⅜in (8mm) from the edge. Trim the allowance to ¼in (6mm) and fold the right sides together. Stitch again, ⅜in (8mm) from the edge, and press.

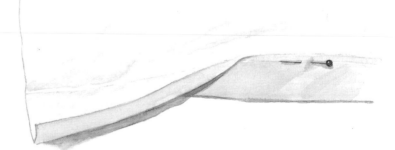

DOUBLE HEM

A double hem consists of one narrow and one deeper turn or two equal turns, which give a firmer edge to fine fabrics. Press the two folds under. Pin and baste, then either machine stitch, catching both folds, or, if you are making a curtain, herringbone stitch by hand.

MITERED CORNER

When two hems meet at right angles, the surplus fabric is finished with a miter to avoid bulk. Press the turns under, then unfold. Fold each corner inward and press so the creases line up to make a square (as shown). Refold the hems, then slipstitch the folded edges together (see below). For a double hem, unfold the second turn only before refolding and stitching.

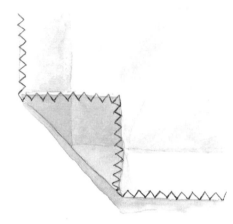

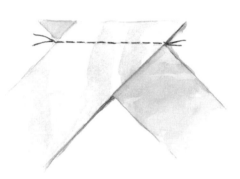

SLIPSTITCH

Slipstitch is used to join a miter or two folded edges, or to secure a folded hem. Bring the needle out through the fold and pick up two threads on the other side. Pass it back through the fold for ¼in (6mm) and repeat to the end.

BIAS STRIPS

Flexible strips of fabric, cut across the grain, are used to cover piping cord. Mark a diagonal line on the fabric at 45 degrees to the edge. Draw a series of lines parallel to this and cut

along them. With right sides together, sew strips at right angles to one another (see above), ½in (1cm) from the edge, to make up the required length, then press the seams open.

JOINING PATTERNED FABRIC

When you are joining lengths of patterned fabric for a curtain or other larger project, the design should match horizontally across the seam. Make sure that each piece starts at the same point on the design as you cut them out. Press under one seam allowance and pin the fold to the second piece so the patterns line up. Join with a long slipstitch. Fold right sides together and machine stitch along the basted line.

With the right side out, fold the strip around the cord. Pin and baste in place ⅛in (3mm) from the cord.

EMBROIDERY STITCHES

If you want to embroider your fabric creations, there is a wealth of stitches to choose from. Here are some of the most useful and easy to do. They can be used for monograms, lettering, filling outlined motifs, or adding color and detail to a plain background.

Threads come in various textures and weights and a rainbow of colors. Tapestry yarn, the heaviest, can be used for stitching on wool fabric as well as canvas. Pearl cotton is thick and lustrous. Flower thread is the finest. Stranded cotton or silk floss consists of six loosely twisted threads that can be used together for a bold look or separated for detailed work.

Match your needle to the thread: a thick chenille needle for wools, a long-eyed crewel needle for stranded floss, or a sharp for fine, single-stranded threads. If you are working on a large piece of fabric, mount it in a hoop or frame to keep the tension, and your stitching, even.

CHAIN STITCH

Chain stitch is a flexible stitch that can be worked in curved or straight lines or in rows as a filling. Insert the needle where it last came up, looping the thread around it from left to right. Bring the point out over the loop, then insert it at the same point, making another loop. Continue this way, anchoring the final loop with a short stitch.

LAZY DAISY STITCH

You can work several single chain stitches in a circle to make a dainty 1930s-style flower. Start in the center, insert the needle at the same point, and bring it out over the thread, creating a loop around it from left to right. Fasten the loop with a small straight stitch, then repeat for the remaining petals.

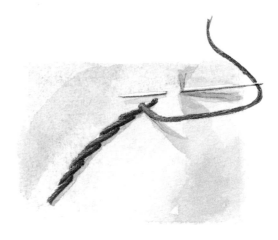

STEM STITCH

As its name suggests, stem stitch is the ideal stitch for flower stalks and tendrils. Working from left to right, make a straight stitch and bring the needle out halfway along and to the left. Repeat, following the line of the design.

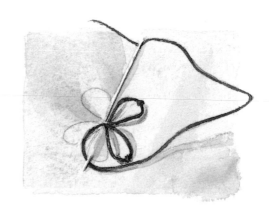

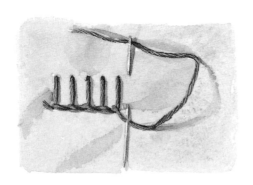

BLANKET STITCH

Traditionally worked in wool to finish the edge of wool fabrics, blanket stitch is also useful for outlines and securing appliqué shapes. Start on the lower line or the edge of the fabric. Insert the needle up to the right and bring it out below with the thread looped below the point. Continue working from left to right, and finish off with a short stitch over the final loop.

FEATHER STITCH

This pretty looped stitch was traditionally used to decorate children's clothes and in conjunction with smocking. Bring the needle up to the right of center, insert it back through the fabric to the right, on the same level, and bring it out diagonally below to the left. Pull through over the thread you have just stitched and insert the point to the left, on the same level. Bring it up diagonally to the right below the starting point and over the thread. Repeat these two steps.

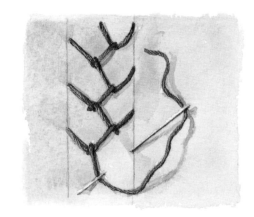

HERRINGBONE STITCH

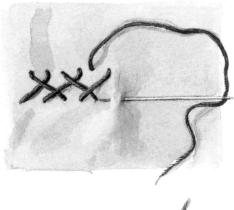

Herringbone is a border stitch that works well as a decorative finish on flat seams, particularly for crazy patchwork and appliqué. Make a diagonal stitch up and work a small horizontal stitch to the left. Make another diagonal stitch down to the right and another horizontal stitch to the left. Repeat these two steps to continue.

SATIN STITCH

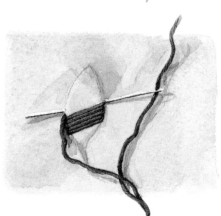

When worked as shown (left), satin stitch is a filling stitch, but it is also useful as a border—worked at right angles between two parallel lines—or for monograms. Starting at the widest point of the shape, work a series of diagonal straight stitches, leaving no space between them, then fill in the remainder.

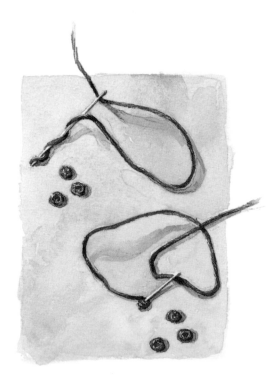

FRENCH KNOTS

This classic filling stitch takes practice to get right. Don't wrap the thread too tight or pull it too hard—or you will get a real knot. The stitch looks best worked in thick thread. Bring the needle up through the fabric, then point it down toward the point from which it emerged. Wrap the thread twice around the needle and, pulling it gently to keep the tension, push the needle back down at same point.

PATCHWORK

Originally patchwork was a thrift craft, born of necessity at a time when new cloth was expensive and hard to come by. A thriving tradition today, it is still the ideal way to use small scraps of fabric to make something new and beautiful.

There are two main methods: machine piecing (used for the baby quilt on pages 68–71), where squares and triangles of fabric are joined to form geometric blocks, and hand piecing, where paper templates are used. Hand piecing is more time-consuming, but it is worked in your lap, making it perfect for occupying winter evenings in front of the fire.

Hexagonal patchwork uses a single, six-sided motif, giving an all-over honeycomb effect. With a clever choice and imaginative arrangement of fabric, you can create intricate kaleidoscopic patterns and rosettes, such as the traditional Grandmother's Flower Garden quilt on page 25 and the table cover on page 76.

HOW TO HAND PIECE

1 Trace this hexagon template and use it as a guide for cutting the backing papers (you can recycle old envelopes or letters written on paper of a heavy weight).

2 Cut out the fabric pieces, following the template and allowing at least an extra ⅓in (1cm) seam allowance all around. Line one side up against the grain of the fabric and make sure any motifs or designs lie in the middle.

3 Baste the paper centrally to the wrong side of the fabric. Working one side at a time, turn back and baste down the seam allowance, sewing through the paper template.

4 To join, hold two hexagons with right sides together and join the two top edges with small overstitches worked through the folds. Take care not to catch the paper with the point of the needle. Join a third patch to adjacent sides of the first and second patches.

5 To make a rosette, sew six patches around a contrasting center. Several of these can then be joined to make an all-over pattern—or you can continue adding concentric circles of hexagons to increase the size. Remove the basting and papers when the work is complete.

resources

Vintage fabrics and vintage-style fabrics can be found everywhere, from thrift stores and flea markets to specialized suppliers. Here is a selection of resources.

ANTIQUES AND FABRICS

A Victorian Elegance
P.O. Box 2091
Plant City, FL 33564-2091
800-660-3640
www.victorianelegance.com
Vintage and antique clothing and accessories.

A Vintage Wedding
www.vintagewedding.com
Offshoot site of A Victorian Elegance; perfect source for period gifts and inspiration; includes sewing patterns.

ABC Carpet & Home
881–888 Broadway
New York, NY 10003
For a store near you,
call 561-279-7777
www.abchome.com
Exotic collection of home furnishings, fabrics, carpets, and accessories.

American Quilts
P.O. Drawer 200
Upton, KY 42784-0200
877-531-1691
www.americanquilts.com
Antique, Amish, and custom-made quilts.

Bloomingdales
1000 Third Avenue
New York, NY 10022
212-705-2000
www.bloomingdales.com
Department store; 24 locations nationwide.

Calico Corners
203 Gale Lane
Kennett Square, PA 19348
800-213-6366
www.calicocorners.com
Retailer of fabric by designers such as Waverly and Ralph Lauren. Stores nationwide. Mail order.

Elegant Era's
105 Oak Rim Ct #15
Los Gatos, CA 95032
www.tias.com/stores/elera/
Fabulous selection of lingerie, lace, silk, linen, jewelry, and more from late 1800s to 1940s.

The Fabric Center
485 Electric Avenue
Fitchburg, MA 01420
978-343-4402
Decorator fabrics at discounted prices. Mail order.

Hancock Fabrics
2605A West Main Street
Tupelo, MS 38801
662-844-7368
www.hancockfabrics.com
America's largest fabric store.

Keepsake Quilting
Route 25B
P.O. Box 1618
Center Harbor
NH 03226-1618
800-865-9458
www.keepsakequilting.com
Quilting fabrics and threads.

Laura Ashley Home Store
171 East Ridgewood Avenue
Ridgewood, NJ 07450
201-670-0686
For a retailer near you,
call 800-367-2000
www.laura-ashleyusa.com
Floral, striped, checked, solid cottons.

Macy's
800 BUY-MACY
www.macys.com
Department store; locations nationwide.

Neiman Marcus
For nearest store, call 888-888-4757
For mail order, call 800-825-8000
www.neimanmarcus.com
Department store; 31 locations nationwide.

On Board Fabrics
Route 27, P.O. Box 14
Edgecomb, ME 04556
207-882-7536
www.onboardfabrics.com
Everything from Balinese cottons to Italian tapestry and woven plaids.

Oppenheim's
P.O. Box 29, 120 East Main Street
North Manchester, IN 469-62-0052
800 461 6728
Country prints, denim, chambray, flannel fabrics, and mill remnants.

Pieces of History Antique Linens
76 Cherry Hollow Road
Nashua, NH 03062
www.tias.com/stores/kayhless
Sheets, tablecloths, napkins, pillows, bedspreads, and much more.

Reprodepot Fabrics
917 SW 152nd Street
Burien, WA 98166
www.reprodepotfabrics.com
Reproduction vintage fabrics.

Salsa Fabrics
3100 Holly Avenue
Silver Springs, NV 89429
800-758-3819
www.salsafabrics.com
Original fabrics in cotton, silk, and wool from Guatemala and Indonesia.

Silk Trading Co.
360 South La Brea Avenue
Los Angeles, CA 90036
800-854-0396
www.silktrading.com
More than 2,000 silk fabrics; nine stores nationwide.

Thai Silks!
252 State Street
Los Altos, CA 94022
800-722-7455
www.thaisilks.com
Silk, velvet, organza, jacquard, and taffeta. Mail order.

RIBBONS, TRIMS, & ACCESSORIES

Britex Fabrics
146 Geary Street
San Francisco, CA 94108
415-392-2910
www.britexfabrics.com
Wide variety of ribbons, trims, notions.

The Button Emporium & Ribbonry
914 S.W. 11th Avenue
Portland, OR 97205
503-228-6372
www.buttonemporium.com
Vintage, jacquard, metallic, wired, and assorted ribbons.

Hyman Hendler and Sons
67 West 38th Street
New York, NY 10018
212-840-8393
www.hymanhendler.com
Novelty and vintage ribbons and trims.

Restoration Hardware
935 Broadway
New York, NY 10011
212-260-9479
www.restorationhardware.com
Not just hardware; funky furnishings and accessories.

The Ribbon Club
P.O. Box 699
Oregon House, CA 95962
530-692-3014
www.theribbonclub.com
Ribbons, trims, tassels, stamens, and packages for creating flowers.

The Ribbonerie Inc.
191 Potrero Avenue
San Francisco, CA 94103
415-626-6184
www.theribbonerie.com
Extensive collection including wired, grosgrain, metallic, and velvet.

Tinsel Trading Co.
47 West 38th Street
New York, NY 10018
212-730-1030
Vintage to contemporary trims.

ONLINE RESOURCES

www.curioscape.com
*Over 40,000 addresses of stores selling
antiques, including textiles and vintage
clothing throughout the country.*

www.ebay.com
*Internet auctions; every category
of merchandize represented.*

www.fleamarketguide.com
*Listings of flea markets held
throughout the country.*

www.marybethtemple.com
*Linens from the Victorian era through
the 1950s; vintage fabrics and trims.*

www.vintagefiberworks.com
*Vintage clothing, accessories, fabrics,
and home decor.*

www.rustyzipper.com
*Vintage clothing from 1920 to 1980,
including fabrics and sewing patterns.*

www.tias.com
*Vast selection of antiques and
collectibles, including textiles.*

FLEA MARKETS

Alameda Swap Meet
South Alameda Boulevard
Los Angeles, CA 90021
213-233-2764
*Seven days a week from 10 a.m.
to 7 p.m. year round, 400 vendors.*

Brimfield Antique Show
Route 20
Brimfield, MA 01010
413-245-3436
www.brimfieldshow.com
*Brimfield is renowned as the outdoor
antiques capital of the world; show held
for a week in May, July, and September.*

Denver Indoor Antique Market
1212 South Broadway
Denver, CO 80210
303-744-7049
Open seven days a week.

Merriam Lane Flea Market
14th and Merriam Lane
Kansas City, KS 66106
913-677-0833
*Open-air market where estates are
bought and sold; weekly in spring
and summer from 7 a.m. until dark.*

Ruth's Flea Market
Highway 431
Roanoke, AL 36274
334-864-7328
*Over 300 booths selling all types of
collectibles; weekly on Wednesday
and Saturday.*

Sullivan Flea Market
Heights Ravenna Road
5 Miles West of Ravenna Center
Ravenna, MI 49451
616-853-2435
*Mix of antiques, collectibles, and
fresh produce; held weekly on Monday
from April to the end of October.*

Tesuque Pueblo Flea Market
Route 5
Santa Fe, NM 87501
505-660-8948
*Focuses on Native American crafts,
antiques, rugs, collectibles; monthly
Friday–Sunday. Call to verify dates.*

Traders Village (Houston)
Eldridge Road
Houston, TX 77083
713-890-5500
*Largest marketplace on the Texas Gulf
coast, with over 800 dealers and over
60 acres of bargains. Open year-round
Saturday and Sunday, 8 a.m. to 6 p.m.*

picture credits

1 Lucy and Marc Salems' London home; **2–3** Francesca Mills' house in London/1970s scarf cushions from Maisonette; **4a** owner of Adamczewski, Hélène Adamczewski's house in Lewes/antique Provençal quilt from Housepoints/cushion made with antique fabric by Caroline Zoob/painting by Tom Hammick; **4bl** Sasha Gibb, colorist, interior consultant and designer/painting by Sasha Gibb/Christmas angel designed and made by Caroline Zoob; **4bcl** Francesca Mills' house in London/coat from Steinberg & Tolkein; **4bcr** Rose Hammick's home in London/antique fabric bags from VV Rouleaux/two bags on right from Grace & Favour/gingham roses in bowl from VV Rouleaux; **4br** Rose Hammick's home in London/hotwater bottle cover from Tobias & the Angel/top eiderdown from Braemar Antiques/middle eiderdowns from Kim Sully Antiques/quilt from Louise Bell; **5l** interior designer Sue West's house in Gloucestershire/pink mug and toile-edged towels from Grace & Favour; **5cl** designer Caroline Zoob's workroom; **5cr** designer Caroline Zoob's home in East Sussex/selection of cushions made from antique fabrics by Caroline Zoob; **5r ph** Simon Upton; **7 ph** Polly Wreford; **8** Rose Hammick's home in London/cushion from Grace & Favour/covered box from Braemar Antiques/quilt made by Lucinda Ganderton; **10** both designer Caroline Zoob's workroom; **11** studio of Sasha Gibb, colorist, interior consultant and designer/covered chair, handwork and printed length by Sasha Gibb; **12–13** all designer Caroline Zoob's workroom; **14l ph** Tom Leighton; **14r** Adamczewski, Hélène Adamczewski's shop in Lewes/apron made by Lattika Jain; **15 & 16l** designer Caroline Zoob's workroom; **16r ph** James Merrell; **17al ph** Tom Leighton; **17bl & r** designer Caroline Zoob's workroom; **18ph** Tom Leighton/ antique silks from Catherine Nimmo; **18–19** cushions by Sasha Gibb, colorist, interior consultant and designer; **19 inset ph** Tom Leighton; **20l** customized crochet throw with sequins by Lucy Salem/vintage velvet pincushions from Lucy Salem; **20c ph** Verity Welstead; **20r–23** studio of Sasha Gibb, colorist, interior consultant and designer/ covered chair, handwork, cushions and printed length by Sasha Gibb; **24 & 25l** the home of Patty Collister in London, owner of An Angel At My Table/hatboxes from Kim Sully Antiques; **25c&r** the home of Patty Collister in London, owner of An Angel At My Table/framed lace from Tobias & the Angel/vintage floral cushions with velvet flowers by Lucy Salem; **26a&bl ph** Polly Wreford; **26r & 27** Rose Hammick's home in London/ armoir from Mark Maynard Antiques/antique toile panel from Nicole Fabre Antiques/ painting by Tom Hammick/purple cushions from Grace & Favour/floral cushions from Lucy Salem; **28 ph** Polly Wreford/an apartment in New York designed by Belmont Freeman Architects; **29** Francesca Mills' house in London/cushions from After Noah; **30** Lucy and Marc Salems' London home/painting by Rachael Garfield/velvet cushions with tassel trim by Lucy Salem; **31** Lucy and Marc Salems' London home/customized crochet throw and striped chair by Lucy Salem/chainlink uplighter by Marc Salem; **32b** the home of Patty Collister in London, owner of An Angel At My Table/cat from Tobias & the Angel; **32r** interior designer Sue West's house in Gloucestershire/selection of cushions on sofa made by Sue West; **33** interior designer Sue West's house in Gloucestershire/blind made from tea towel-style fabric from The Housemade; **34l** owner of Adamczewski, Hélène Adamczewski's house in Lewes/print by Tom Hammick; **34r ph** Christopher Drake/Ali Sharland's house in Gloucestershire; **36–37** designer

Caroline Zoob's home in East Sussex/selection of cushions made from antique fabrics by Caroline Zoob; **38–39** owner of Adamczewski, Hélène Adamczewski's house in Lewes/antique Provençal quilt from Housepoints/cushion made with antique fabric by Caroline Zoob/painting by Tom Hammick/basket by door from Housepoints; **40** cushion made by Lattika Jain; **42l** cushion made by Greta Zoob, Caroline Zoob's mother-in-law; **42–43 & 43** designer Caroline Zoob's home in East Sussex/selection of cushions made from antique fabric by Caroline Zoob/blind made from antique linen; **44l** Sasha Gibb, colorist, interior consultant and designer/cushions and window seat cover by Sasha Gibb; **44r** Claudia Bryant's house in London/vintage cushions by Claudia Bryant; **45** Sasha Gibb, colorist, interior consultant and designer/cushions by Sasha Gibb; **46** Rose Hammick's home in London/French antique sheet awning form Kim Sully Antiques, patchwork quilt by Emily Medley/shawl and flip-flops cushion from Grace & Favour/ bed from Litvinof & Fawcett; **47** Rose Hammick's home in London/patchwork quilt by Emily Medley/hotwater bottle covers from White & Gray; **48–49** Rose Hammick's home in London/cushion from Grace & Favour/covered box from Braemar Antiques/quilt made by Lucinda Ganderton; **50** Lucy and Marc Salems' London home/vintage fabric compositions by Lucy Salem; **51l** the home of Patty Collister in London, owner of An Angel At My Table/dressing table from An Angel At My Table/curtain from Lucy Salem/quilt from Nicole Fabre/two bags from Grace & Favour; **51r** cream rose from Grace & Favour/red rose from VV Rouleaux; **52** Lucy and Marc Salems' London home/floral cushion by Lucy Salem; **53** Rose Hammick's home in London/hotwater bottle cover from Tobias & the Angel/top eiderdown from Braemar Antiques/middle eiderdowns from Kim Sully Antiques/quilt from Louise Bell; **54l** Rose Hammick's home in London/covered box from Braemar Antiques/button bag from An Angel At My Table; **54r** Claudia Bryant's house in London/dress from Louise Bell; **55r** patchwork bag made from antique quilts and ticking by Sue Holley of Susannah in Bath; **56** café curtain made from children's hankies by Lucinda Ganderton; **58l ph** James Merrell/eiderdown from Tobias & the Angel; **58r ph** James Merrell; **59** Lucy and Marc Salems' London home; **60l** Sasha Gibb, colorist, interior consultant and designer/blanket blinds by Sasha Gibb; **60–61 & 61** designer Caroline Zoob's home in East Sussex/lampshade an original design by Caroline Zoob; **62–63** all interior designer Sue West's house in Gloucestershire/cushions and lampshades from The Housemade; **64–65** Sasha Gibb, colorist, interior consultant and designer/blankets and child's coat from Sasha Gibb, cowgirl bag and cowboy laundry bag made by Emily Medley; **66a** the home of Patty Collister in London, owner of An Angel At My Table/bear far left from Kim Sully Antiques/middle bear from Tobias & the Angel/baby shoes from Grace & Favour/ painting from An Angel At My Table; **66b p**h Debi Treloar/Sue & Lars-Christian Brasks' house in London designed by Susie Atkinson Design; **67l&c ph** Debi Treloar; **67r** 1920s night-dress envelope from a P & A Antiques collectors fair stall; **68** quilt made by Lucinda Ganderton/cushion made by Sasha Gibb; **72a** pan-holder made by Lattika Jain; **72b & 73** Claudia Bryant's house in London/glove from Grace & Favour, lined with Liberty print fabric/apron made by Emily Medley/fabric on table from Mad Fashion Bitch/cushion and mugs from After Noah/stools from Ed; **74** Claudia Bryant's house in London/apron made by Emily Medley; **76** owner of Adamczewski, Hélène Adamczewski's house in Lewes/antique patchwork quilt from Grace & Favour; **77a** both owner of Adamczewski, Hélène Adamczewski's house in Lewes/antique ticking on table and in cupboard from Kim Sully Antiques/all ceramics from Adamczewski; **77b ph** Simon Upton; **78l** Rose Hammick's home in London/checked sofa cover and red toile cushion from Nicole Fabre/1920s gold cushion from Kim Sully Antiques; **78r** felt place mats made by Sasha Gibb/egg cosies made by Cecilie Telle; **79** Rose Hammick's home in London/French enamelled tins from Grace & Favour/1950s curtains from Alexandra Fairweather; **80** both Lucy and Marc Salems' London home/free-standing 'retro' kitchen by Marc and Lucy Salem; **81l** owner of Adamczewski, Hélène Adamczewski's house in Lewes/antique checked voile curtain from Kim Sully Antiques; **81r** the home of Patty Collister in London, owner of An Angel At My Table/cafetière warmer made by Cecilie Telle; **82l** interior designer Sue West's house in Gloucestershire/tablecloth by The Housemade; **82r & 83** the home of Patty Collister in London, owner of An Angel At My Table/jug cover from the Dining Room Shop/place mats from Tobias & the Angel; **84** both designer Caroline Zoob's home in East Sussex/patchwork curtains made by Caroline Zoob from antique fabric; **85 ph** Caroline Arber/Linda Garman's home in London; **86l ph** Simon Upton; **86r** interior designer Sue West's house in Gloucestershire; **87** interior designer Sue West's house in Gloucestershire/linen-covered notebooks and napkin box with initial from The Housemade; **88** owner of Adamczewski, Hélène Adamczewski's garden in Lewes/peg bag made by Lattika Jain; **89l** hangers and lined basket from Louise Bell; **89r** the home of Patty Collister in London, owner of An Angel At My Table/pile of 1950s fabrics from Lucy Salem; **90l** floral sachet made from 1970s fabric from Flirty Flowers on 1970s scarf from Chi Chi Ra Ra; **90r ph** James Merrell; **91l** retro laundry bags from The Laundry; **91c** lavender bag from Susannah/retro bedlinen from The Laundry; **91r** hanger from Susannah; **92l** Lucy and Marc Salems' London home/bathroom organizer by Lucy Salem; **92r** the home of Patty Collister in London, owner of An Angel At My Table/bags made by Cecilie Telle; **93l** Lucy and Marc Salems' London home; **93r** Claudia Bryant's house in London/vintage fabric-lined towel from Lucy Salem; **94l ph** Tom Leighton; **94r ph** James Merrell; **95** interior designer Sue West's house in Gloucestershire/pink mug and toile-edged towels from Grace & Favour; **96–97** designer Caroline Zoob's home in East Sussex/floral dorothy bag made by Caroline Zoob; **100 ph** Pia Tryde/the garden of Vanessa de Lisle, fashion consultant; **100–101 ph** Pia Tryde; **102 & 103al ph** Pia Tryde; **103bl&r ph** Polly Wreford/Mary Foley's house in Connecticut; **104** lace from Caroline Zoob; **105a** boat card made by Holly Tree Cards from Housepoints; **106** Sasha Gibb, colorist, interior consultant and designer/painting by Sasha Gibb/Christmas angel designed and made by Caroline Zoob; **107l** Francesca Mills' house in London/Christmas stocking designed and made by Caroline Zoob; **107r** wire wreath decorated with glass flowers and leaves by Lucy Salem; **108l** Francesca Mills' house in London/ starched crocheted doilies by Lattika Jain; **108c** stocking cards from Susannah; **109l** Claudia Bryant's house in London/stocking made by Sasha Gibb; **110l** interior designer Sue West's house in Gloucestershire; **110r** owner of Adamczewski, Hélène Adamczewski's garden in Lewes/framed embroidered picture designed and made by Caroline Zoob; **111 inset** boat card made by Holly Tree Cards from Housepoints; **112 ph** Polly Wreford; **113l** bag from VV Rouleaux; **113r** bag from Grace & Favour; **114b** lace from Caroline Zoob; **114c ph** Polly Wreford; **114r & 115** Francesca Mills' house in London/opera coat from Steinberg & Tolkein; **116l** basket from Susannah; **117a** Edwardian evening bag from Kim Sully Antiques; **117b** lace from Caroline Zoob; **118b ph** James Merrell; **128** Louis the dog in basket lined with 1960s fabric/basket from Chairworks.

In addition to those mentioned above, we would like to thank all the people who kindly allowed us to photograph their homes including Mr & Mrs Derald Ruttenberg, Russell Glover and Angela Miller, and Katie Fontana and Tony Niblock.

designers whose work is featured in this book

ph = photographer, a = above, b = below, r = right,
l = left, c = center.

Adamczewski
88 High Street
Lewes
East Sussex RN7 1XN
UK
+44 (0)1273-470105
adamczewski@onetel.net.uk
Pages **4a, 14r, 34l, 38–39, 76, 77a, 81l,
88, 110r.**
Fine housewares.

An Angel At My Table
116A Fortess Road,
Tufnell Park,
London NW5 2HL
+44 (0)20-7424-9777
and
14 High Street
Saffron Walden
Essex CB10 1AY
+44 (0)1799-528777
Pages **24, 25, 32b, 51l, 54l, 66a, 81r, 82r,
83, 89r, 92r.**
Painted furniture and accessories.

Susie Atkinson Design
+44 (0)468-814134
Page **66b.**

Belmont Freeman Architects
Project Team: Belmont Freeman (principal designer),
Alane Truitt
Sangho Park
110 West 40th Street
New York, NY 10018
212-382-3311
Page **28.**

Claudia Bryant
+44 (0)20-7602-2852
Pages **44r, 54r, 72b, 73, 74, 93r, 109l.**

Sasha Gibb
Interior and color consultant
+44 (0)1534-863211
home@sashagibb.co.uk
Pages **4bl, 11, 18–19, 20r–23, 44l, 45, 60l,
64–65, 68, 78r, 106, 109l.**
*Contemporary home furnishings designed and
made from vintage blankets.*

Russell Glover
Architect
russellglover@earthlink.net
Pages **58r, 118.**

The Housemade
Sue West
Interior & product design
+44 (0)1453-757771
sue.west@btopenworld.com
www.avaweb.co.uk/coachhouse.html
Pages **5l, 32r, 33, 62–63, 82l, 86r, 87, 95, 110l.**

Lattika Jain
+44 (0)20-8682-3088
Pages **14l, 40, 72a, 88, 108l.**
Freelance in textile design, fashion & knitwear.

Emily Medley
Designer
emilymedley@mac.com
Pages **46, 47, 64–65, 72b, 73, 74.**

Francesca Mills
Designer/Stylist
+44 (0)20-7733-9193
Pages **2–3, 4bcl, 29, 107l, 108l, 114r, 115.**

Plain English Kitchen Design
The Tannery
Tannery Road
Coombs
Stowmarket
Suffolk IP14 2EN
UK
Page **86l.**

Lucy Salem
+44 (0)20-8563-2625
lucyandmarcsalem@hotmail.com
Pages **1, 20l, 25c&r, 27, 30, 31, 50, 51l, 52,
59, 80, 89r, 92l, 93l, 93r, 107r.**
*Makes and sources soft furnishings and decorative
items for the home.*

Sharland & Lewis
45 Long Street
Tetbury
Gloucestershire GL8 8AQ
UK
+44 (0)1666-502440
Page **34r.**

Cecilie Telle
cecilietelle@hotmail.com
+44 (0)20-7272-1335
Pages **78r, 81r, 92r.**
*Makes felted wool products for children, women,
and men, and for the kitchen.*

Caroline Zoob
For commissions, please ring +44 (0)1273-479274.
Caroline Zoob's work is also available at:
Housepoints
48 Webbs Road
London SW11 6SF
UK
+44 (0)20-7978-6445
Pages **4a, 4bl, 5cl&cr, 10, 12–13, 15, 16l, 17bl&r,
36–37, 38–39, 42–43, 60–61, 84, 96–97, 104,
105a, 106, 107l, 110r, 111 inset, 114b, 117b.**
*Housepoints sells painted furniture, decorative antiques
and vintage treasures, original design pillows, and framed
pieces from antique textiles.*

index